I0482823

CEO Guide to Doing Business in Russia

By Ade Asefeso MCIPS MBA

Second Edition

ISBN-13: 978-1500100575

ISBN-10: 1500100579

Publisher: AA Global Sourcing Ltd
Website: http://www.aaglobalsourcing.com

Table of Contents

Disclaimer

This publication is designed to provide competent and reliable information regarding the subject matter covered. However, it is sold with the understanding that the author and publisher are not engaged in rendering professional advice. The authors and publishers specifically disclaim any liability that is incurred from the use or application of contents of this book.

If you purchased this book without a cover you should be aware that this book may have been stolen property and reported as "unsold and destroyed" to the publisher. In this case neither the author nor the publisher has received any payment for this "stripped book."

Dedication

This book is dedicated to the hundreds of thousands of incredible souls in the world who have weathered through the up and down of recent recession.

To my family and friends who seems to have been sent here to teach me something about who I am supposed to be. They have nurtured me, challenged me, and even opposed me.... But at every juncture has taught me!

This book is dedicated to my lovely boys, Thomas, Michael and Karl. Teaching them to manage their finance will give them the lives they deserve. They have taught me more about life, presence, and energy management than anything I have done in my life.

Chapter 1: Introduction

Russia is the largest country in the world. It is the eighth largest retail market in the world and the fourth-largest market in Europe. Despite slowing growth, and reduced public and private investment programmes, opportunities do remain due to the Russian oil and gas boom.

It remains a long term market of great potential for British exporters and investors. UK-Russia economic relations remain strong.

Russia is the UK's fastest-growing major export market and the third-largest export market outside Europe and North America, with favourable cross-sector opportunities, some unique in scale. The government's economy modernisation and infrastructure development agenda, underpinned by 140 million consumer's appetite for quality services and goods, produces a need for international expertise and products.

UK exports to Russia in 2011 increased by 39% from 2010, and equalled £4.78 billion. Since 2001 UK-Russia trade has been growing by an average of 21% year on year.

Why Russia?

Western goods and expertise remain in demand. The most promising opportunities for foreign companies are in the Advanced Engineering, Financial Services,

ICT, Power/Energy, Sports and Leisure Infrastructure (particularly the Sochi 2014 Winter Olympics), Airports, Construction, Creative Industries, Rail and Water.

Geography

The Russian Federation stretches across Eurasia from Eastern Europe to the Pacific coast. After the collapse of the Soviet Union, Russia became the largest country in the world in terms of territory.

Population

The population of the Russian Federation is approximately 143 million. Although approximately 80% of the country's population is ethnically Russian, the Russian Federation is a multinational state and is home to numerous ethnic minority groups, including sizeable Tatar (3.8%) and Ukrainian (2%) populations. Roughly 73% of the population lives in urban areas and 12 cities have a population of over 1 million. The largest city in Russia is Moscow, with a population of approximately 10.6 million, followed by St. Petersburg, with a population of approximately 4.6 million.

Economy

The 8 years of Vladimir Putin's presidency from 2000 to 2008 coincided with an era of rapid economic growth fuelled by sky-high commodity prices and accompanied by a significant increase in living standards. The government's devaluation of the ruble during the 1998 financial crisis gave local producers significant advantages over their foreign competitors. Local consumption was boosted by the introduction of consumer loans and mortgages. Among the other drivers of economic growth was an increase in the utilization of industrial capacity constructed in the Soviet period. Between 1999 and 2007 GDP rose by an average of 6.8% annually. Real fixed capital investments increased by an annual average of 10% between 2000 and 2007, while real personal incomes rose at an average annual rate of 12%.

Over these years Russia successfully paid off a substantial portion of its foreign debt and amassed the third largest foreign currency reserves after China and Japan. These achievements, in conjunction with prudent macroeconomic policies and renewed government efforts to advance structural reforms, have raised business and investor confidence, with new business opportunities emerging in such sectors as telecommunications, retail, pharmaceuticals and the power industry in particular.

In 2008-2009 Russia was severely hit by the international financial crisis. A slump in commodity prices, collapse in the financial markets, restricted access to external financing, rising unemployment and a consequent drop in internal consumption shook the foundations of the Russian economy. In 2009 GDP contracted by 7.9%, while industrial output fell by 10.8%.

Since the outbreak of the crisis the government has increased its efforts to safeguard the economy. The

9

Central Bank implemented a step-by-step ruble devaluation which prevented panic and an eventual bank run. The government has proposed bail-out initiatives for the economy's largest companies with a view to limiting the negative social impact of massive lay-offs. Some banks and financial services companies have been acquired by government-controlled organizations. A package of tax initiatives encouraging economic activity has been adopted.

During 2010-2011 the Russian economy seemed to had stabilized. In 2011 Russia's gross domestic product grew by 4.2 percent, the world's third highest growth rate among leading economies. The government expects it to grow 3.7 percent in 2012. Global demand and commodities prices are likely to be the biggest factors affecting the Russian economy in the coming years.

Chapter 2: 2018 World Cup Opportunities in Russia

Russia will host some of the biggest sporting events in the world in the next few years. The list includes the 2018 football World Cup and the 2014 Winter Olympic Games.

The investment planned for these sporting events is huge, with trade experts estimating the World Cup to be worth £35bn and the Sochi Winter Olympics £20bn.

Russia has revealed that its preliminary budget for holding the 2018 FIFA World Cup is almost twice what it projected when it won the bid in 2010.

Sports Minister announced a budget of 600bn roubles (£12bn; $19bn), nearly 40% of which will go into building or renovating stadiums. The rest of the money will be spent on transport and hotel infrastructure.

Russia beat off rival bids from England and other EU states to host the world's highest-profile single sports event. Mr Mutko said the costs were expected to be split evenly between the public and private sectors.

Eleven host cities have been chosen which span the European part of Russia; Moscow (with two of the 12 stadiums), St Petersburg, Sochi, Yekaterinburg,

Kazan, Nizhny Novgorod, Rostov-on-Don, Samara, Kaliningrad, Volgograd and Saransk.

The FIFA World Cup 2018 will be the culmination of a series of high profile sporting events hosted by Russia. It comes immediately after the centenary of the 1917 revolution and just over a quarter of a century after the collapse of the Soviet Union. Billions of people will tune in for the football tournament. In addition to the VIPs and the world media, hundreds of thousands of sports fans will come here in effect Russia will welcome the world onto its soil in a way that has never happened before in the history of the country.

About 40 percent of the £12 bln budget will pay for sports facilities. Moscow will have two venues; the 90,000-seat Luzhniki stadium, which will stage the final and 45,000-seat Spartak stadium. Five of the 12 stadiums that will host the 64 matches are already under construction in Moscow, St.Petersburg, Kazan, Sochi and Saransk. Design of four more stadiums - in Volgograd, Nizhny Novgorod, Rostov-on-Don and one more city that has yet to be determined will be commissioned imminently. The remaining two arenas will be commissioned in 2013.

60 percent of the proposed budget will go towards building and improving airports, hotels and roads, as well as to provide medical and communications services and security.

Making an impact for the Business

The London 2012 / Sochi 2014 Olympics link gives the UK a unique advantage in sports business in this market and a series of high level official and ministerial exchanges between the two countries before the end of the year will give further opportunities to reinforce these messages.

Visits in both directions by business and host officials will also be important if we are to maximise the opportunities. Although 2018 may seem some way off the key period for winning infrastructure contracts will be in the next 18 months.

And British firms should be handily placed after delivering the London 2012 Olympic Games to provide the expertise needed to host these major sporting contests.

Both of the two Russian headline events, the World Cup and Winter Olympics as well as other sporting tournaments will need new stadiums and associated infrastructure. Russian biathelete Olga Zaitseva The Olympic baton has passed to Russia for the 2014 Winter Games in Sochi.

Business opportunities for foreign firms around these events could include sectors such as architecture, engineering, construction management, transport, security, environmental planning, power engineering and sports venue "fitting out" - providing plant and equipment, seating, surfacing, lighting and IT.

At the latter stages of event preparation there are further opportunities; things such as security, recruitment, volunteering programmes, training, broadcasting, event management, media signage, ticketing, screens, temporary overlay, crowd control, transportation and branding.

And finally, during the actual events there will also be openings in hospitality and catering.

The World Cup in 2018 provides opportunities not only in one geographic region, but across the country, with a dozen or so cities hosting the football tournament.

Hosting Fifa's showpiece event means transport links in Russia will need to be upgraded, including doubling the capacity at Moscow's three airports, as well as major improvements to transport in Moscow and St Petersburg.

Thousands of kilometres of new roads and rail are required as well as high-speed rail links between the host cities, which will be announced later this month.

Meanwhile, the Russian government also plans to invest £6.5bn to develop its tourism infrastructure and to create 19,000 additional hotel rooms.

Russia offers a really big number of opportunities in many other industries such as oil and energy. With all the changes being made, Russia is expected to offer a much better infrastructure for companies and investors interested in the country which may lead to an array of post event opportunities. Of course everybody involved in the business world is aware of what the opportunities may be, and the intent of this book is to bring some other areas that may not be as clear as others.

Chapter 3: 2014 Winter Olympic Opportunities in Russia

The Russian government is using the 2014 Games as a catalyst for development of the city of Sochi, the 1000-km of the Russian Black Sea coastline, and the whole region of Krasnodar Krai.

The long-term aim is to boost the local tourism industry, which is currently largely domestic, by delivery of improved facilities on the coast-line and the world-wide exposure the 2014 Winter Games will generate.

The opportunities are enormous, from construction, engineering, environmental technologies and hospitality, through to logistics, security, IT and creative industries.

Opportunities

On 4 July 2007, the International Olympic Committee announced that Sochi Olympic and Paralympic Winter Games will take place in Sochi from 7 to 23 February, the 2014 Paralympic Games - from 7 to 16 August.

The slogan of the Olympic Games in Sochi is "Gateway to the Future" with the aim to:
1. Transform Sochi into a year-round tourist destination.
2. Develop Russia's first world-class ski resort.

3. Create a centre for winter sports in Russia.
4. Establish Russia's first alpine, sliding and ski jumping centre.
5. Implement Russia's new philosophy of investing domestically for the future.

Olympic opportunities for foreign are enormous; key areas are detailed below.

Construction

The official delivery plan records some 218 projects to be constructed in Sochi. More than 1 trillion roubles (C USD 35 billion) will be spent between 2009 and 2012 on the preparations for the 2014 Winter Olympic Games with 699.3 billion roubles (C USD 23.31 billion) allocated from the federal budget.

The projected budget for construction of 12 custom-built sports venues, located in two clusters (the "Coastal Cluster" for ice events and the "Mountain Cluster" in Krasnaya Polyana) is about 200 billion roubles (C USD 6.6) billion. The operating budget for the actual games is USD 1.8 billion.

The biggest spending was planned for 2010, RUR 348.7bn (C USD 11.6billion), including RUR 228 billion (C USD 7.6 billion) from the federal budget. 2011 spending was planned at RUR 307 billion (C USD 10.2 billion) and in 2012, at RUR 216.5 billion (C USD 7.21 billion).

Construction on some venues, like the skating and curling centres, have already started, while the Alpine slopes have all been designed and prepared. Construction on all other venues will have start in the first quarter of 2010.

More than 70 test events in different sports will be held in 2012 and 2013. About 80% of the venues needed for the 2014 Games will be built from scratch. The ratio between public and private investment into the Olympic projects is expected to be 70:30. Currently the key private sector investors are Gazprom, Interros, Sberbank, Rosneft and Russian Railways.

Gazprom's spending on preparations for the Sochi Olympics is the largest of all the investment plans for the 2014 Winter Games. The company intends to invest RUR 68 billion (C USD 2 billion) in the construction of facilities for the 2014 Winter Olympic Games in Sochi by 2012. RUR 28 billion (C USD $ 930 million) of this sum was invested by Gazprom in 2009. Gazprom's investment targets include a skiing complex, a four-star 600-beds hotel for skiers 1,500 meters above the sea level and a new gas pipeline with an annual capacity of 3.27 billion cubic meters.

Housing

For the Sochi Games two Olympic villages will be constructed, the main of them will be situated at the Black sea coast, the additional in mountains. For accommodation of visitors and participants of the Sochi Games it is planned to create 6,348 five-star rooms, 17,483 four-star rooms, 24,016 three-star rooms and 9,052 two-star rooms.

According to the forecast of social and economic development in 2009 – 2011 more than 2.1 mln sq m of housing in Sochi should be constructed. The housing in the city will then increase from 18.2 sq m per person in 2007 to 20.8 sq m in 2011 and the construction in the city will reach 500 – 700 thousand sq metres a year. By 2032 the personal space of each inhabitant of Sochi will make already 32 metres, and all existing available housing will increase from 7,330 to 20,080 sq metres.

Sixteen new hotels will also be built, while 10 existing ones will be remodelled. Sochi is virtually doubling in size to meet the new demands for 2014 and beyond. Its expansion is aimed at increasing tourism industry from current USD 5 billion to USD 8-10 billion after 2014.

Total camping capacity should grow by 2032 up to 220 thousand places. The number of health-resort visitors will reach eight millions.

The boarders of the city will change: Sochi will expand from 17,677 to 22,236 hectares by reduction of the former farmlands and State forest fund.

Infrastructure

The plan requires delivery of complex infrastructure projects, including more than 100km of railway lines, 75km of highways, 19 flyovers, 20 tunnels, 5,000m of mooring installations, a new waste processing plant, and a port for a capacity of 10 ships and 300 yachts, plus goods terminals and port stations.

Airport capacity is doubling to take 2,500 passengers an hour. 37 km of temporary technical roads have been laid, 10 temporary bridges across the Mzymta River have been put to commission as well. Over 9 thousand people are working now at the construction of an integrated motor and railway road Adler-Krasnaya Polyana that will link the Mountain and the Coastal clusters. It will be put into commission in 2013.

Construction of 22 out of 26 permanent bridges has already started. The Sea port and the Freight Yard started their operation in 2009.

Airport

Sochi International airport holds the 9th place among the largest airports in Russia, handling over 1.5 million passengers every year. It is currently served by 35 airlines, including Austrian Airlines and Latvian AirBaltic, which now operate regular and charter flights to 50 domestic and international destinations.

Investment in Sochi airport will reach approximately £5.5 billion by 2014. With its two crossed runways, Sochi airport is now able to handle all but the largest commercial aeroplanes being used in Russia and abroad. Fully-equipped permanent aircraft storage areas can accommodate up to thirty-nine aircraft at the same time.

Handling capacity of the airport is 800 passengers per hour on domestic flights and 130 passengers per hour on international flights. But this will be more than doubled with the opening of the new state-of-the-art terminal.

The new building of the airport was built in 2007 but has not started its operation. The building is over 60,000 square meters in size. Access to the aircraft boarding area is provided by 11 boarding bridges. The parking lot can accommodate up to 1,000 automobiles. The handling capacity is 2,500 passengers per day, of those 2,000 on domestic flights and 500 on international flights.

The top management of the new airport terminal plans that all of the latest in airport technologies will be used in the Sochi airport. Among them; 100% three-tier baggage check and automatic sorting, an integrated safety system, including video surveillance; controlled access; video identification; biometric systems; 24-hour safety monitoring of the terminals.

The airport will also be equipped with modern IT systems meeting the requirements of IATA (DCS, AODB, FIDS, RMS, CUTE-CUSS, e-ticketing and RFID-bag identification). There will be systems integrated to allow passengers with disabilities access to the entire airport. The Sochi airport has positive experience in cooperation with leading international companies on matters of technology.

Railway

The state company Russian Railways is playing a major role in preparing Sochi for the Olympic Games. A specialised railway will be created to connect the Olympic Park, the airport and the venues in Krasnaya Polyana. Russian Railways plan to improve access to Sochi by establishing a high-speed Moscow-Adler link (capable of speeds of 200 km/h), thanks to which travelling from Moscow to Sochi will take just 15.5 hours. Stations are being modernised for people with disabilities.

Cross-sectoral opportunities

Contracts arising from the Games cover all sectors, from architecture, engineering, construction management, transport, security, environmental planning, power engineering, sport venue fit out, plant and equipment, seating, surfacing, lighting, IT, through to event delivery (security, recruitment, volunteering programmes, training, broadcasting, event management, media signage, ticketing, screens, temporary overlay, crowd control, transportation and branding), hospitality and catering.

There has been identified a particular interest in foreign companies providing newest technologies in construction, design and engineering services, project management, security equipment and security control management, legal advice, sound and broadcasting equipment, telecommunication equipment, environmental friendly vehicles, special equipment for the Paralympic Games and disabled people, as well as education services.

The Olympic Legacy

A sustainable legacy is one of the strategic goals of the Sochi 2014 project. The core concept around the programme "The Olympic Legacy" is for creation of sports legacy to develop Sochi as a sport centre. It is aimed for the development of business and cultural tourism for the low season. There are also plans to grow Sochi as a recreational and educational centre.

The big Sochi territory is bigger than Moscow. It is planned to zone the city and develop each zone according to various strategies.

1. Lazarevskaya is a very important region of the Big Sochi. It will be developed into a traditional family resort featuring inexpensive cosy hotels, paid parking places, the middle price service and the clean sea. It is planned that the resort will get more than one million tourists and relieves the central part of the Big Sochi.

2. The central part is a respectable area where the new quay will be built. It will become the centre for evening entertainment with a lot of greenery, bars and restaurants.

3. Adler should remain a big tourist centre, where small private hotels and large hotels will be situated.

4. Imeretinka is the only place in Sochi where the beach is sandy. Luxurious five-star hotels will be situated at the seaside, a little further

four and three-star hotels. One of the best in Europe and in the world amusement park and the year round congress expo-centre will be built there.After the Olympic Games it is planned to use the Olympic stadium as a football arena, the skating centre as an exhibition centre, the Ice Palace of sports as the business and exhibition centre.

5. Krasnaya polyana is Russia's first world-class ski resort. Bobsleighing track, "Rosa Khutor", "Alpika-Service", "Khrebet Psehako" complexes and the curling arena will be used as the national training base and the venues for international competitions.

Chapter 4: Political System in Russia

The Russian Federation is a federal republic consisting of 83 constituent entities. There are six categories of federal constituent entity which, while subtly different in classification, are constitutionally defined as equal members of the federation. The 21 republics (corresponding to the homelands of various ethnic groups) enjoy a certain degree of regional autonomy. The federation is further divided into 46 oblasts (regions), one autonomous oblast (autonomous region) and 9 krais (territories) in which 4 autonomous okrugs (autonomous districts, also delineated for various ethnic groups) are located. Moscow and St. Petersburg are classified as cities of federal significance. In 2000, Russia was further divided into seven federal super-districts (circuits) with the aim of ensuring federal supervision over regional affairs.

Each constituent entity of the federation possesses its own charters, political institutions and local legislation. Approximately half of the constituent entities have signed bilateral treaties regulating the relationship between the regional and federal governments.

Significant progress has been made towards greater consistency between the regional and federal legal systems. However, when conducting business transactions at the regional level treaty stipulations should be carefully reviewed as they may assign slightly different rights and privileges to the constituent entity in question.

Constitutionally, the President of the Russian Federation is elected for a six year term (which was extended from four to six years in 2008). Any given individual is limited to two terms in succession. The President is vested with extensive powers, serving as the head of state, the commander-in-chief of the armed forces, and the highest executive authority of the federation. The office of the President also includes the powers of decree, legislative veto, and the power to appoint and dissolve the Government. The President is primarily responsible for domestic and foreign policy and represents Russia in international relations. Furthermore, as of December 2004 the President was granted the authority to directly appoint Russia's regional leaders, subject to confirmation by the regional legislature. The procedure was amended in December 2008; according to the new law the political party that has obtained a majority in the regional legislature submits 3 candidates for the President's consideration.

The Prime Minister oversees the activities of the government and serves as the acting President if the President becomes ill and is unable to carry out the functions of that office. The Prime Minister's authority as acting President expires upon the election of a new President, which would normally be three months after the former President's authority expired.

Since the election of Vladimir Putin to the Russian presidency in May 2000, the country has undergone a number of sweeping political reforms aimed at centralizing power within the federal executive. Mr. Putin was re-elected in March 2004. In March 2008 Putin's designated successor, Dmitry Medvedev, won the general election with an overwhelming majority. In May 2008 Vladimir Putin was appointed Prime Minister. On 4 March 2012, Mr. Putin won the 2012 Russian presidential elections in the first round.

Legislative power is exercised by a bicameral Federal Assembly, which consists of the Federation Council (upper house) and the State Duma (lower house). Since January 2002 the Federation Council has consisted of two representatives from each federal constituent entity, one from the executive branch appointed by the regional governor, and one from the legislature nominated by the regional assembly.

This has changed from the previous system in which leaders of the regional legislative and executive branches served on the council ex officio. The State Duma consists of 450 members elected nationwide by proportional representation though party lists. Previously 225 of the 450 members were elected in single member constituencies; however in December 2004 these seats were abolished.

The first election under the new rules was held in December 2007. In addition, new rules were introduced governing national political parties, increasing both the minimum number of party members required for registration (from 10,000 to

50,000) and the threshold to secure Duma seats (from 5% to 7% of the national vote).

The lowest governmental level in the Russian Federation is local self government. Reformed in September 2003, bodies at this level remain relatively new and untested. Current law distinguishes between community-level government and the governments of towns and villages, reforming the roles and responsibilities of each level. However, the overall influence of local self-government depends on how much authority has been delegated to the local level by the regional government. Foreign investors should be aware of the position of local bodies in regions where they conduct business since these bodies may possess limited powers of taxation.

At the top of the Russian judicial system are three high courts: the Constitutional Court, Supreme Court and Supreme Arbitrazh (Commercial) Court. The 19 judges of the Constitutional Court review all constitutional disputes. The Supreme Court reviews civil, criminal, and administrative disputes involving private individuals, while the Supreme Arbitrazh Court reviews commercial disputes and administrative disputes involving legal entities and individual entrepreneurs. Judges for all of these courts are appointed for life by the Federation Council on the recommendation of the President.

Chapter 5: Russian International Relations

Russia is still in the process of defining its position in the post-Cold War world. One of the primary accomplishments of Russian foreign policy has been an improved relationship with Western Europe and the United States, although this bond has been severely tested on several occasions. In the past few years Russia has been re-evaluating its foreign policy agenda in response to increased Western involvement in both Eastern Europe and Central Asia.

One of the key pillars of Russian foreign policy has been the Commonwealth of Independent States (CIS), whose membership is comprised of most of the former Soviet republics. Since 1991 the CIS has struggled to establish itself as an effective and integrated body.

Currently, the most significant issue facing the CIS is the establishment of a "Common Economic Space" between Russia, Ukraine, Belarus, and Kazakhstan. Agreement in principle was announced in 2003, mandating the creation of a self-governing supranational commission on trade and tariffs. The ultimate goal is the creation of a regional organization with the ability to expand its membership and forge a currency union, the first stage of which was scheduled to begin in 2005. In August 2008, following an escalation of hostilities between Russia and Georgia over the separatist region of South Ossetia, Georgia withdrew from the CIS.

Recently Russia has been very active in various Western programs, including the strengthening of the International Non-proliferation Initiative as well the formation of a joint Russia-NATO action plan on international terrorism, which envisages the exchange of confidential information as well as joint exercises and anti-terrorism training.

Internationally, Russia continues to be an active member of all bodies of the United Nations and retains a permanent seat on the Security Council with veto rights.

Russia has always had close ties with its neighbour and major trading partner – Belarus. In 1997 a supranational entity, the Union of the Russian Federation and the Republic of Belarus, was formed. However, since then the initial enthusiasm for integration has waned and a union with a single currency remains merely a project.

Chapter 6: Overseas Business Risk in Russia

Vladimir Putin won the Presidential elections on 4 March 2012 with 64% of the vote and was inaugurated as President on 7 May 2012. He has appointed the former President, Dmitry Medvedev, as his Prime Minister.

Russia's economy remains in good short term health with consensus expectations for GDP growth this year of around 3.5 - 4%. The budget is close to balanced and unemployment and inflation are at historic lows. However, commentators continue to warn that economic and institutional reforms are needed for the economy to achieve its full potential and reduce its vulnerability to global commodity price changes.

These reforms include modernising and diversifying the economy; improving investment, innovation and the business environment, notably by tackling corruption and reducing the role of the state; and reorient spending towards healthcare, education and infrastructure. The makeup of the Government's cabinet will give an indication of how Russia intends to tackle these issues.

Oil and gas are at the heart of the Russian economy, responsible for around 25% of GDP, 50% of Federal budget revenues and 80% of exports. The Russian real economy has recovered from the dramatic falls of

2009 and the IMF currently predicts GDP growth at 4% and 3.9% in 2012 and 2013 respectively. The 2011 World Bank's Ease of Doing Business survey ranks Russia 120th out of 183 countries, indicating significant bureaucratic challenges in the business environment.

Bribery and Corruption

Corruption is a major barrier to business in Russia. Business concerned that situation is deteriorating. Medvedev has made tackling corruption a major part of his modernisation agenda but most Russians are sceptical of short-term change.

Corruption is endemic in Russia. Transparency International ranks Russia 143 out of 182 countries in its Corruption Perceptions Index in. Anti-corruption lobby group "Clean Hands" estimate that the level of bribes is as much as half of Russia's GDP.

This damages Russia's economic development. BNP Paribas estimate that perceptions of corruption costs Russia the equivalent of 4 per cent of GDP in lost foreign investment each year. The general public identified it as the biggest block to economic growth in a recent survey by independent pollsters Levada Centre. The Association of European Business agrees; "extras" can account for 20% of the cost of doing business in Russia.

Business representatives report that the situation is deteriorating. IKEA and Daimler have both been caught up in high profile corruption scandals, with

IKEA having threatened to suspend further investment as a consequence. Even the Ministry of Interior estimates that the average size of a bribe has increased five-fold in the last two years.

Overseas corruption also hurts honest companies and raises the costs of doing business. Surveys regularly show that a significant number of UK companies have lost business to a bribing competitor or turned down overseas opportunities due to overseas corruption.

Russian buildings

President Medvedev has made the fight against corruption a key element of his Modernisation Agenda. Building on Putin's Anti-Corruption Commission, established in 2004, he introduced a National Plan to Counteract Corruption only a month after taking office. New legislation came into force on 10 January 2009, requiring civil servants (and spouses) to disclose all income and assets, putting in place a framework for determining conflicts of interest, and simplifying the Criminal Code to hold corrupt judges to account.

Russia also has international commitments: to the Council of Europe's Criminal Law Convention on Corruption since 1999 and the UN's Counteraction to Corruption (UNCAC) since 2006. The OECD Working Group on Bribery is considering a phased approach to Russia's bid for membership, contingent on tackling three issues; criminalising foreign bribery;

clarifying the liability of legal persons; extending the statute of limitations.

Despite the flurry of activity, Medvedev's initiatives have had little traction to date. Analysts argue that the problem is not with the legislation but with its implementation. Some officials apparently agree. Russian Prosecutor-General, Yuri Chaika, claimed that Russian law-enforcers were only rooting out minor cases of bribery, ignoring large-scale corruption, while many believe the corruption cases brought by the authorities are little more than a pretext to dismiss officials who have fallen out of favour.

In the absence of effective action by the State, some businesses have adopted their own approaches. In 2010 at least 40 German companies operating in Russia signed up to an Anti-Corruption Pact, governed by Swiss law. British companies are subject to the UK Anti-Bribery Act.

Visit the Business Anti-Corruption portal which provides advice and guidance about corruption in Russia.

Terrorism Threat

There is a high threat from terrorism. Attacks cannot be ruled out and could be indiscriminate, including in places frequented by expatriates and foreign travellers. Attacks have occurred most frequently in Moscow and in some regions of the North Caucasus particularly Dagestan and Chechnya.

In Moscow, terrorist groups have carried out suicide attacks in public places, including the Metro system and airports. The risk of terrorism could rise quickly in relation to any escalation of violence in the North Caucasus.

The security situation in the North Caucasus remains unpredictable. Because of the threat from terrorism and kidnappings.

There are protective security issues attached to doing business in Russia; business people need to be conscious of the following activities of the local security service (FSB):

1. IT attacks against office computers, laptops, PDAs and other electronic devices.
2. Physical, audio and video surveillance.
3. Approaches to staff.
4. Interception of telephone calls (landline and mobile), texts, emails, fax and post.
5. Searches of offices, homes, vehicles and (especially) hotel rooms (including safes).

Businesses can reduce the risk to themselves, their employees and customers by remaining vigilant, being security minded and having good security measures in place.

You should try to reduce the vulnerability of your business and staff to national security threats, including those such as terrorism, cyber-attack or espionage.

The most effective way to secure your business against these is to use a combination of measures covering physical, personnel and information security including cyber security.

Physical security

Physical security is important in protecting against a range of threats and addressing vulnerability. You should put in place security measures to remove or reduce your vulnerabilities to as low as reasonably practicable, bearing in mind the need to consider safety as a priority at all times.

Advice on Physical security measures is provided on ways to protect buildings, contents, equipment and so on. These include basic good housekeeping, CCTV/intruder alarms/access control systems, parking and traffic controls, mail screening and lighting.

Personnel security

Personnel security is a system of policies and procedures which seek to manage the risk of staff or contractors exploiting their legitimate access to an organisation's assets or premises for unauthorised purposes. These purposes can encompass many forms of criminal activity, from minor theft through to terrorism.

The CPNI website includes guidance on how such risks, including those from "insiders", can be minimised. It also covers pre-employment screening, personal document verification, security culture, ongoing personnel security measures and personnel risk assessments.

Some Russians complain that international investors focus too much on Russia's risks while ignoring similar risks in other markets. For example, Russia gets demerits because it repealed of many of the glasnost-era freedoms but China's repression is overlooked. The Russian resentment is probably valid, but even so, Russia has plenty of risk:

An aging population and brain drain: The average age of the population in Russia is 38.5 years, and the birth rate is below the replacement rate. This situation raises the question of whether Russia will have enough workers to support its retirees and enough workers and consumers to support a more diversified economic base. On top of the declining birth rate, Russian scientists and engineers have a long history of leaving for greener pastures in other countries. However, as Russia's economy becomes more stable, the people will feel more confident about the future, which in turn will boost the birth rate (the government already pays a bonus to women who have a second child) and lower migration.

Corruption and crime

Like many formerly Communist countries, Russia has a long-standing culture of corruption because that's how people got things done. That corruption scares off foreign investors. The government has been addressing the issue, and if investors notice a real change, Russia will become a more attractive place to do business.

Reliance on one key industry

The Russian economy is based on oil and gas. That's good because global demand for carbon-based fuel is huge and growing. However, by being so narrowly focused, the Russian economy is directly exposed to price fluctuations. Also, the planet's oil and gas will be used up someday. The lack of diversity in Russia's economy creates a big challenge over the long-term.

On the plus side, Russia has the potential to have a more diverse economy. It has a range of natural resources and geography, and its people are talented. Diversification should happen.

Intellectual Property

IP rights are territorial, that is they only give protection in the countries where they are granted or registered. If you are thinking about trading internationally, then you should consider registering your IP rights in your export markets.

Chapter 7: The Russian Soul

That is something that you feel immediately when you arrive in Russia, even in Moscow; Russians are not Westerners. The term Russian soul has been used in literature to describe Russian spirituality.

The Russian soul can be described as a cultural tendency of Russians to describe life and events from a religious and philosophically symbolic perspective. Whether this is true or not can be challenged by the fact that younger Russians are strongly influenced by globalization and economic development opportunities. Nevertheless Russians are really proud and appreciate the arts and rich history of Russia. Russians are almost always very educated, whilst in most Western countries only 50-60% of people receive University Education. Russians always have an opinion about politics and current affairs. So it's good for you to understand that education is a value, rather a necessity.

Russians do not tend to make a distinction between hard logic and emotion, which governs the Western culture. They value intuition rather than rationality. They will make business with you because they like you, not because of economical or technical arguments based on rational analysis.

The Oligarchs

The Oligarchs, the billionaires who, through the use of legal and illegal methods concentrated large fortunes during the transition from Communism to Capitalism, have given a false impression about doing Business in Russia. Some of them have the largest business and personal divorces in the world. Other have used prostitution rings to make their business, while others have been accused for killing, stealing and anything else illegal. These figures however are hated within Russia. The fact that the money was stolen, result on them not being idolized, as it happens with many Western businessmen. So, during a business relationship, this topic could be an ice maker (rather than an ice breaker).

Chapter 8: Business Etiquette in Russia

Political changes, government reforms, a stable economy, vast natural resources and a large population have all led to Russia seeing enormous advances in their foreign trade links. However, Churchill's description of the country as a 'riddle wrapped in a mystery inside an enigma' still very much holds true for outsiders looking in. Gaining some basic insight into the Russian mentality, culture and etiquette are key for anyone doing business in Russia.

Russians will do business with you because they like you. This means that, even though a business meeting will always start in formal ways, a business will develop only through the creation of informal bonds. In other words, even though in the beginning of a relationship they might appear 'cold' and reserved, they are much happier in an environment where they can also express their feelings and emotions. That's why meetings might last longer than expected; It's much more important to complete the business through a good hand shaking rather stick to timetables.

Other things to consider when doing business in Russia

Russians do not value without culture behaviour. So, don't swear, don't forget to leave your coat in the cloakroom, don't stand with your hands in the pockets, and do not shout in public.

Do not start with a joke. Instead, keep your presentation serious, include facts and technical details. You can inject emotion in your discussion slowly. In my personal experience humour is rarely translated and what makes some people laugh in one culture may offend people from different countries.

Even though it's not of primary importance, your personal network matters as well. So use it and refer to it accordingly.

Meetings can be interrupted and remain formal. Moreover, egalitarianism is crucial here: Nobody is better than anybody else.

Constant communication through visits and phone calls are crucial. Moreover, when a business has been set up, monitoring the performance is critical.

Bring gifts with you. Russian people value gifts. Good gift ideas are brand-name products of high quality. With home visits try flowers, alcohol and branded food products. Avoid cheap products; they can have a negative impact in your relationship

Meeting and Greeting

The typical greeting is often a (very) firm handshake with the appropriate greeting for the time of day - dobraye utra (good morning), dobryy den (good afternoon) or dobryy vecher (good evening).

Even though it may sound a bit stiff it is commonplace when doing business in Russia to introduce yourself using only your surname. Before meeting your Russian counterpart ensure you find out if there are any titles they use as these are extremely important and should be used. If you are visiting Russia it is appropriate to refer to your counterpart by either "gaspodin" (a courtesy title similar to "Mr.") or "gaspazhah" (similar to "Mrs." or "Miss") plus his or her surname.

On the whole Russians have three names. The first name is the given name while the last name is the father's family name. The middle name is a version of the father's first name, known as a patronymic; for a man, it ends with the suffixes "vich" or "ovich" meaning 'son of.' For a woman, the patronymic is also the father's first name but with suffixes "a" or "ova" added, which means 'daughter of.'

When doing business in Russia make sure you take a business card. It is always a good idea if you plan to maintain contacts in Russia to have one side translated into Russian. If you do so make sure you add your title and any degrees or qualifications you have.

Meetings and Negotiating

Always be punctual when doing business in Russia. However do not take offense if your Russian counterpart is not. It is not unknown for Russian business people to turn up hours late. A good indication of how serious a meeting is taken is how punctual they are.

Initial meetings are usually approached as a formality. It is at this stage that your credibility will be assessed. The best strategy is to appear very firm and dignified, while maintaining an air of warmth and approachability.

Pitches or presentations should be simple and straightforward. Generally Russians are not impressed by foreigners doing business in Russia who use special visuals, flashy PowerPoint presentations and the like. These do not sway decisions. The most critical element is demonstrating your knowledge, professionalism and expertise.

Many Russian business personnel speak good English so presenting in the language is not a problem. If it could be then hire a Russian interpreter. It is however that you make the effort to present anything written in Russian.

Negotiations are an interesting affair for anyone doing business in Russia. They are tough and like to indulge in a fair amount of theatre if necessary. Their main aim is to gain concessions so there will be a lengthy process of grinding you down. Caving in too early is a sign of weakness so stand your ground. If you do feel the need to concede ask for the gesture to be reciprocated in some way. Generally speaking, Russians view compromise as a sign of weakness. Don't be surprised by loss of tempers, walkouts, threats to end the deal, and similar incidents. It's all part of the fun.

Re-negotiations are always present, so even though you will have a contract, expect the unexpected.

Entertaining

Doing business, conducting meetings, making decisions, negotiating and getting to know each other are increasingly being done at dinner. If your Russian counterpart decides to invite you out do not refuse the request as it would be rude.

At the table centre seats are used by the most senior attendees. As a guest you should be sat in the middle opposite your immediate counterpart.

Remember Russians do like a drop or two of alcohol. Refusing to drink is unacceptable unless you give a plausible excuse, such as explaining that health or religious reasons prevent you from imbibing. Always bear in mind that you may be discussing so know your limit.

Chapter 9: Promoting Foreign Investment in Russia

The Constitution and the Civil Code of the Russian Federation, as well as laws on joint stock and limited liability companies and insolvency, provide the general legal framework for trade and investment in Russia.

Foreign investments are regulated by the Federal Law On Foreign Investments in the Russian Federation, dated 9 July 1999 (the "Law on Foreign Investments"). The Law on Foreign Investments guarantees foreign investors the right to invest and to receive revenues and profits from such investments, and sets forth the terms for foreign investors' business activity in Russia.

The Law on Foreign Investments does not apply to the investment of foreign capital in banks, credit organizations, insurance companies or non-commercial organizations; foreign investments in such entities are regulated under different Russian legislation.

The objective of the Law on Foreign Investments is to attract foreign materials, financial resources, and technology and management skills to improve the Russian economy, while providing stability for foreign investors.

The Law on Foreign Investments emphasizes the role of both federal and regional legislation, and stipulates that foreign investors and investments must be treated no less favourably than domestic investments, with certain exceptions. Such exceptions may be introduced to protect the Russian constitutional system, the morality, health and rights of persons, or in order to ensure state security and defence.

The Law on Foreign Investments permits foreign investment in most sectors of the Russian economy: portfolios of government securities, stocks and bonds, direct investment in new businesses, the acquisition of existing Russian-owned enterprises, joint ventures, etc. Foreign investors are protected against nationalization or expropriation unless such action is mandated by a federal law. In such cases, foreign investors are entitled to receive compensation for any investment and other losses.

One of the most important features of the Law on Foreign Investments is the tax stabilization clause, also known as the "Grandfather Clause", set forth in Article 9. This clause applies to.
1. Foreign investors that are implementing "priority investment projects".
2. Russian companies with more than 25% foreign equity ownership.
3. Russian companies with some foreign participation that are implementing "priority investment projects."

Article 2 defines a priority investment project as a project with foreign investment of at least RUB1 billion (about USD33.3 million at the current exchange rate), or where a foreign investor has purchased an equity interest of at least RUB100 million (about USD3.3 million at the current exchange rate); in either case, the investment project must also be included in a list of projects approved by the Russian Government.

For companies and projects that qualify, the Grandfather Clause prohibits increasing the rates of certain import duties and federal taxes until initial investments have been recouped (up to a maximum of seven years, unless this period is extended by the Russian Government). Key exceptions to the Grandfather Clause are established for protective customs tariffs on commodities, excise tax, VAT on domestic goods, and Pension Fund payments. Article 9.4 provides a further and potentially broad exception for laws protecting certain public or state interests. Article 9.5 contemplates the adoption of regulations to implement the Grandfather Clause. Despite all these exceptions and qualifications, it remains arguable whether the tax stabilization clause is of real benefit to foreign investors.

Restrictions on Strategic Companies

Certain restrictions on foreign investments are imposed by Russian Law No. 57-FZ of 29 April 2008 "On the Procedures for Foreign Investments in Companies of Strategic Significance for National Defence and Security" (the "Law on Strategic Companies"). The Law on Strategic Companies is designed to regulate the acquisition of control over

Russian strategic companies by foreign investors or "groups of persons" that include a foreign investor. Acquisitions by such entities of control of strategic companies (including through acquisitions of shares) require the preliminary consent of the Russian Government and/or a post-transaction notification.

The Law on Strategic Companies provides a list of more than 40 activities that constitute strategic activities in Russia. Accordingly, any company engaged in such activities is viewed as a strategic company. Strategic activities include the following:
1.   Works having an active impact on geophysical processes.

2.   Works related to hydro-meteorological processes and events.
3.   Activities related to the use of infectious agents.

4.   Activities related to the nuclear industry and the storage of nuclear and radioactive materials.

5.   Activities related to encryption and licensed encryption techniques, excluding distribution and maintenance of encryption techniques and related services performed by Russian banks that are not directly owned by the Russian Federation.

6.   Activities related to the secret obtaining of information in premises and equipment (excluding activities performed for the purposes of the security of legal entities).

7.   Activities related to the production, trade, repair and utilization of weapons and military equipment, and their spare parts and ammunition (excluding bladed weapons, civil and service weapons) and explosive materials for industrial purposes.

8.   Activities related to aviation equipment and security.

9.   Space activities.

10.   Activities related to television or radio broadcasting on a territory, where half or more of the population of a constituent entity of Russia.

11.   Services provided by a company included in the register of natural monopolies, (excluding natural monopolies in the public telephone and wireless communication and postal communications fields, and services for the supply of heat energy and electrical energy through the distribution grid).

12.   Activities performed by a company included in the register of companies having more than a 35% market share in a particular market of goods and occupying a dominant position in the following fields:
a.   The market of communication services on the territory of Russia (excluding providing access to the Internet).
b.   The market of fixed telephonic communication on the territory of five or more constituent territories of Russia.

c.   The   market   of   fixed   telephonic communication on the territories of Moscow and St. Petersburg.

13.   Activities related to geological research of subsoil and/or mineral exploration and extraction of federal subsoil.

14.   Procurement of aquatic biological resources (fishing).

15.   Performance of printing by a commercial entity, if such commercial entity is capable of printing no less than two hundred million pages a month.

16.   Performance of editorial office activities and/or activities of a periodical publisher, publishing publications with individual circulations of no less than one million.

Therefore, from the standpoint of foreign investment, it is important to verify all activities the target company is engaged in to assess whether it qualifies as strategic and is therefore subject to the restrictions outlined below.

Controlled Transactions

The following transactions involving the acquisition of control over strategic companies require the preliminary consent of the Russian Government:
  1. Transactions   with   shares   (participatory interests) if as a result of such transactions a foreign investor or group of persons acquires:

2. The right to direct or indirect disposal of 25 or more percent of the total number of votes at shareholder level for companies using federal subsoil plots.
3. The right to direct or indirect disposal of more than 50 percent of the total number of votes at shareholder level for companies engaged in strategic activities other than the use of federal subsoil plots.
4. The right to appoint
    a. the chief executive officer, and/or
    b. more than 50 percent of the members of a collective executive body of the strategic company;
5. The unconditional ability to elect more than 50 percent of the members of the board of directors (supervisory council) or another collective governing body of such company.
6. For companies using federal subsoil plots transactions aimed at the acquisition by a foreign investor/group of persons of shares (participatory interests) if the foreign investor or group of persons already has.
    a. The right of direct or indirect disposal of twenty five or more percent of the total number of votes at shareholder level (that is, any increase in a shareholding in a strategic company).
    b. The right to appoint the chief executive officer, and/or twenty five or more percent of the members of a collective executive body of such a company.

c. The unconditional ability to elect twenty five or more percent of the members of the board of directors (supervisory council) or other collective governing body of such company.

7. Agreements resulting in the acquisition by a foreign investor or by a group of persons of rights to perform the functions of a management company.

8. Other transactions aimed at the acquisition by a foreign investor or group of persons of the right to determine the decisions of the governing bodies of such a company, including the rights to determine its business activities; and/or

9. Transactions aimed at the acquisition by a foreign state, international organization or organization controlled by them, of the right to dispose directly or indirectly of more than Five percent of the total number of votes at shareholder level for companies using federal subsoil plots; or More than 25 percent of the total number of votes at shareholder level for companies engaged in strategic activities other than the use of federal subsoil plots.

Similar criteria are employed by the Law on Strategic Companies when defining the notion of "control". "Control" denotes not only a certain minimum shareholding level, but also rights to appoint management bodies and otherwise determine the company's business activity.

Acquisition of five percent or more of the shares (whether voting or not) in any strategic company requires providing a post transaction notification to the Federal Antimonopoly Service.

Special Restrictions for Foreign States, International Organizations and Organizations under Their Control

Investments of foreign states, international organizations and organizations under their control into Russian companies (strategic and non-strategic) are subject to additional clearance requirements under the Law on Foreign Investments. Any transaction which gives a foreign state, an international organization or an organization under their control the right to control (dispose of) directly or indirectly more than 25% of the total number of votes attached to voting shares in any Russian company, or otherwise block decisions of the governing bodies of a Russian company, requires preliminary clearance from the Russian Government and/or the Federal Antimonopoly Service.

Moreover, a foreign state, international organization or organization controlled by them are explicitly prohibited from acquiring control, as defined by the Law on Strategic Companies, over strategic companies.

Namely, they are not allowed to acquire:
   1. 25 or more percent of the total number of votes at shareholder level for companies using federal subsoil plots;

2. 50 or more percent of the total number of votes at shareholder level for companies engaged in strategic activities other than the use of federal subsoil plots.

Consequences of Violation of the Law on Strategic Companies

Transactions executed in breach of the Law on Strategic Companies are deemed void. The parties to a void transaction may be ordered to return everything received under such transaction in a court action. If it is impossible to reverse a deal, a court may rule to deprive the foreign investor of voting rights at general shareholders meetings of a strategic company if the foreign investor has not complied with the requirements of the Law on Strategic Companies.

Chapter 10: Special Economic Zones in Russia

According to the Law on Special Economic Zones (SEZ), a SEZ is a geographical region in Russia which benefits from a preferential regime for conducting business on its territory, thereby encouraging inward investment. The State provides infrastructure, incentive tax, administrative, and customs regimes for SEZ residents. The benefits of SEZs only apply to foreign investors upon the creation of a Russian subsidiary, as only Russian legal entities may make an application to become a SEZ resident, as per Federal Law 116-FZ of 22/07/2005. The application should be supported by a business plan and submitted to the Ministry for Economic Development of the Russian Federation. The Department of SEZ and Project Finance of the Ministry provides advice on preparing applications.

Types of SEZ:

A number of Technological Implementation Zones are located in the Moscow Region. Dubna focuses on nuclear technology, energy saving, aerospace and civil engineering, Zelenograd focuses on microelectronics, nanotechnologies and medical studies; Elsewhere, the St Petersburg zone focuses on computer programs, databases and complex equipment; while in Tomsk there is zone that focuses on new materials, micro- and nanoelectronics.

Industrial and Development Zones are located in the Lipetsk Region, they focus on consumer appliances, electronics, machinery and construction materials; in Alabuga (the Republic of Tatarstan), they focus on components for the automotive industry and petrochemicals; and in Samara, they focus on automotive components, construction materials, and petrochemicals. Tourism and Recreational Zones are located in the Republics of Altai and Buriatiya, in the Krasnodar, Stavropol and Altai Territories, in the Kaliningrad, Northern Caucasus, and Irkutsk Regions. There is also a newly created Zone on Russkyi Island near Vladivostok.

Port Zones are located at the Ulyanovsk airport and the Seaports in Murmansk and Khabarovskiy Kray. Other zones are currently being examined. The activities to be conducted in PZs will include load discharging, warehouse services, transportation and forwarding, ship chandler services, ship maintenance and technical support, wholesale trade, simple assembling, packaging and marking, procession of sea products and operation and maintenance of the PZ.

Skolkovo Innovation Centre is a Russian version of the "Silicon Valley". The Centre will be based in Skolkovo a town 20 km west of Moscow which currently hosts a prestigious business school. Skolkovo will be declared a special territory to provide favourable conditions for innovative and high-tech research and development. A number of leading international companies have expressed an interest in participating in the project.

Sverdlovsk Special Economic Zone offers a preferential regime for conducting business in Russia. Setting up in the Sverdlovsk SEZ, Russia's titanium valley and the centre of its titanium and steel production, will offer market access benefits to UK companies.

The RF Government is keen to develop the engineering sector in Russia and attract foreign investment. The government seeks to encourage regional and local governments to provide every support to foreign companies localising production or assembly in Russia.

Last year the Russian Government approved the set-up of a Special Economic Zone (SEZ) in the Sverdlovsk Region in the Urals between two leading industrial centres of the region; Nizhny Tagil and Verkhniaya Salda (176 km of Ekaterinburg) in close vicinity to major world titanium producer VSMPO-Avisma and major Russian steel producer NTMC.

The SEZ is intended for any foreign manufacturing companies looking to localise production or assemble in Russia. The companies will enjoy the following benefits:
1. Exemption from property tax and land tax.
2. Reduction of profit tax to 15.5%.
3. Free customs clearance with no import duty.
4. Free from VAT on imported goods and components.
5. Other privileges within the existing law in force.

Infrastructure, utilities supply will be provided at the expense of the Regional Government's budget. The Government will provide guarantees to protect the companies from adverse changes in the current taxation.

Foreign companies who decide to localise production or assembly in the Urals will get direct Government's support and incentives. The chosen territory for SEZ will give a good access to transport infrastructure, materials supply and opportunity to get into supply chains of major Russian companies.

There are 4 such zones in Russia currently.

Russia operates a number of Special Economic Zones (SEZ) which offers benefits for companies locating in these zones. Locating in these zones can enable foreign companies to overcome market access issues in Russia.
1.   Tomsk Special Economic Zone
2.   Samara Special Economic Zone
3.   Sverdlovsk Special Economic Zone (Titanium Valley)

Tomsk Special Economic Zone offers a preferential regime for conducting business in Russia.

Setting up in Tomsk SEZ, one of the leading centres of science and education in Russia will offer market access benefits to foreign companies.

Tomsk Special Economic Zone provides high quality infrastructure, good choice of potential local partners, and well educated human resources with relatively low pay expectations. Tomsk is one of the leading centres of science and education in Russia. There is potential for joint ventures in ICT, biotechnologies and medical, nanotechnologies and new materials sectors.

The priority areas of focus for research and development activity in Tomsk Special Economic Zone are:

Information and communication technologies and electronics.
1. Development and experimental production of firmware for organization of digital television.
2. Development of radio-technical systems.
3. Development of quantum electronics devices.
4. Development of power and high-current electronic devices.
5. Software development.
6. Development and application of software and hardware systems for the automation of technological processes, etc.

Biotechnologies and medicine
1. Medical biotechnologies.
2. Production of diagnostics based on gene engineering.
3. Biologically active substances and drug substances.
4. Industrial biotechnologies.
5. Agricultural biotechnologies.
6. Development of medical devices, etc.

Nanotechnologies and new materials
1. Development of functional and construction nanomaterials.
2. Metal nanopowders and submicron micropowders of inorganic compounds.
3. Nanofibras of inorganic compounds.
4. Development of nanobiotechnology.
5. Development of nanoengineering and nanosystem machinery, etc.

New Samara Special Economic Zone will offer preferential regime for conducting business in Russia.

Setting up in the Samara SEZ, the centre of Russia's automotive and aerospace industry, will offer market access benefits to foreign companies.

The RF Government is keen to develop a competitive automotive sector in Russia. Prime-Minister Putin recently signed the Decree to set up a Manufacturing Special Economic Zone (SEZ) in the Samara Region (Togliatti) to start functioning in 2012.

The Samara Region is the centre for automotive and aerospace industry of Russia. The companies localising their production in SEZ will enjoy the following benefits:
1. Exemption from property tax for up to 5 years.
2. Exemption from the land tax for up to 5 years.
3. Reduction of profit tax to 15.5% for 5 years.
4. Free customs zone for 5 up to 5 years.

5. Other privileges within the existing law in force.

Infrastructure will be built at the Government's budget expense. The Government will allocate about £1.45 million for road building, energy supply facilities and other necessary infrastructure.

Setting up in the Samara SEZ, the centre of Russia's automotive and aerospace industry will offer market access benefits to foreign companies and is an opportunity for foreign companies to enhance their sales in the Russian market. Price is a key element in entering this market and very often sales of foreign goods and services are low in this market because their prices are too high to compete in the market with other suppliers. Production localisation is a way to reduce prices and make them competitive.

Production localisation in Special Economic Zones will enjoy tax privileges and other benefits granted by Russian Government. Given that, the customer base will be ensured too. In other words to run a business in a Special Economic Zone will be less costly than in other parts of Russia. There are 4 such zones in Russia currently.

Chapter 11: Representative Office and Branch of a Foreign Legal Entity

Legal Status

A representative office or a branch of a foreign legal entity is not considered to be a Russian legal entity, but rather a body representing the interests of a foreign legal entity in Russia.

A representative office is entitled to carry out liaison and ancillary functions in order to promote the business of its foreign founder.

Representative offices are not expected to engage in commercial activities in Russia. Consequently, most representative offices are not subject to profits tax, unless their activities give rise to a "permanent establishment" for tax purposes, i.e., when a foreign legal entity engages in regular commercial activity through its representative office (for example, the sale of goods or the provision of services).

A branch is a subdivision of a foreign legal entity, which may fulfil all or part of the functions of its foreign founder. These functions include contracting with Russian entities with payments in foreign currency and rubles, sales and marketing and other business activities.

The obligations imposed on a branch may include the same obligations as imposed on a representative office. However, a branch has less flexibility in selecting an accrediting authority in Russia than a representative office. This can sometimes affect the effectiveness of visa support and other areas.

Registration

There are several bodies authorized to grant accreditation to representative bodies, including those responsible for the accreditation of representative offices in a particular industry; representative offices of foreign banks, for example, are accredited by the Central Bank of the Russian Federation. The bodies most frequently charged with accreditation of foreign entities are the Chamber of Commerce and Industry of the Russian Federation (the "CCI") and the State Registration Chamber at the Ministry of Justice of the Russian Federation (the "SRC").

All documents from a foreign legal entity must be notarized and apostilled/legalized in the country of execution, and any document supplied in a language other than Russian must be accompanied by a translation which has a notarized certification.

Accreditation is usually granted for a period of up to three years, with the right to extension.

Branch offices must be accredited by the SRC in accordance with the 1999 Federal Law on Foreign Investments.

Following accreditation, the representative office or branch office must carry out a number of post-accreditation procedures before it becomes fully operative, including registration with the State Statistics Committee, with the tax authorities, and with the Russian social benefits funds.

Chapter 12: Forming Limited Liability Companies in Russia

Number of Participants

An LLC may be established by one or more persons or legal entities ("participants"). However, if the number of participants exceeds 50, the LLC must be reorganized into an open joint stock company or a production cooperative within a year. An LLC may not have as its sole participant another business entity consisting of a single person.

Rights of Participants

The participants in an LLC have the right to:
1. Participate in the management of the LLC in accordance with the procedures established by the LLC Law and the company's charter.
2. Obtain information concerning the activities of the LLC and have access to its accounting and other documents in accordance with the procedures established by the LLC charter.
3. Participate in the distribution of profits.
4. Sell or otherwise assign their participation interests in the LLC charter capital, or a part thereof, to one or more of the participants in the LLC, and to third parties, unless prohibited by the LLC's charter, in accordance with the procedure established by the LLC Law and the LLC's charter.

5. Receive a portion of the assets left over after settlement with creditors in case of liquidation of the LLC.

The participants in an LLC also have other rights as provided by the LLC Law, and may have additional rights set forth in the LLC charter during the establishment of the LLC, or which are granted at a later date by a decision of the LLC's general participants' meeting. The following points should be noted with regard to granting additional rights to LLC participants:

1. Where additional rights are granted by decision of the LLC's general participants' meeting, this decision must be unanimous; and

2. Additional rights granted to a particular participant in the LLC are not transferred to any party acquiring all (or a part) of such participant's ownership interest if it is transferred.

Obligations of Participants

The participants in an LLC are required to:

1. Make contributions to the charter capital as specified in the LLC Law and the LLC charter (or in the decision on the establishment of the LLC, if there is only one participant in the LLC) and within the time periods specified in the LLC Law; and

2. Not to disclose confidential information concerning the activities of the LLC. Participants in an LLC also have other

obligations as provided for by the LLC Law, and may have additional obligations set forth during the establishment of the LLC in the LLC charter, or which are imposed on them later by a decision of the LLC's general participants' meeting.

The following issues should be considered when imposing additional obligations on participants of an LLC:

1. When additional obligations are imposed by decision of the LLC's general participants' meeting on all LLC participants, this decision must be made unanimously;

2. If additional obligations are imposed by decision of the LLC general participants' meeting on a particular LLC participant, such decision must be made by a two-thirds majority vote of the total number of votes held by the LLC participants, provided that the LLC participant on whom such additional obligations are imposed voted in favour of such decision or consented to such obligations in writing; and

3. Additional obligations imposed on a particular participant(s) in the LLC do not pass to any party acquiring all (or part) of such participant's ownership interest in case it is transferred.

Charter Capital

The charter capital of an LLC consists of contributions made by its participants. The initial charter capital may not be less than RUB10,000 (approx. USD333 at the current exchange rate).

At least 50% of the charter capital amount must be paid up by the date of the LLC's registration, and the balance must be paid in full within the first year of its operation. Contributions may be made in cash or in kind, and certain customs benefits may be available for in-kind contributions made by foreign investors. The charter capital may be increased only after the original charter capital has been paid up in full.

An LLC has to provide access to the information about its net assets to any interested party. The net assets of a company must exceed its charter capital amount. If the LLC has net assets less than its charter capital amount for two years from its establishment and each subsequent year, it must reduce the charter capital to the amount of its net assets. Moreover, if a Russian company has net assets less than the minimum charter capital established by law for two years from the LLC's establishment and each subsequent year, it must take a decision on voluntary liquidation. Failure to take such decision may result in a claim from the Russian tax authorities for the forced liquidation of such company. Also a Russian company with negative net assets may not declare and/or pay dividends to its shareholders.

It should be noted that the charter capital reduction procedure triggers the right of the LLC's creditors to demand acceleration of the LLC's obligations to such creditors.

Participation Interests

A participation interest (i.e., an ownership share) in an LLC is not considered a security under current Russian legislation. Therefore, in contrast to the shares of a joint stock company, LLC participation interests do not need to be registered.

Participation interests in an LLC may be sold to third parties if allowed by the LLC charter, but other participants must be given the right of first refusal to purchase the participation interests at the price offered to the third parties. Participants in an LLC, if allowed by the LLC charter, may have a unilateral right to withdraw from the LLC and to be compensated for their participation interests.

Management Structure

The general participants' meeting is the highest governing body of an LLC. Participants in an LLC may choose to create a board of directors to govern the operations of the LLC.

The General Participants' Meeting has the right to:
1. Amend the charter.
2. Define the basic goals and directions of the LLC.

3. Delegate to a commercial organization or to an individual entrepreneur the authority reserved for the LLC chief executive officer, and approve the agreements with such organizations or persons, if such decision does not fall within the competence of the Board of Directors in accordance with the LLC charter.
4. Assign supplemental rights and duties to the participants in the LLC.
5. Approve the annual financial report and the distribution of profits.
6. Alter the amount of the charter capital of the LLC.
7. Approve regulations governing the internal activities of the LLC; and
8. Reorganize or liquidate the LLC, appoint a liquidation commission, and approve the liquidation balance sheet of the LLC.

The daily management of the LLC is the responsibility of the executive body, which may be one person (the general director) or may consist of both the general director and the management council. The executive body is responsible for all matters that do not fall within the authority of either the board of directors or the general participants' meeting. The general participants' meeting or (if provided by the LLC charter) the board of directors may choose to delegate the powers of the executive body to an external commercial organization or to an individual manager on a contractual basis.

Registration

With effect from 1 July 2002, the Federal Law on State Registration of Legal Entities (the "Registration Law") transferred the authority for registration of legal entities in Russia to the local bodies of the Federal Tax Service of the Russian Federation. As a result, the state registration of legal entities and their registration as taxpayers are now under the auspices of the local tax inspectorates.

The following documents are required for registration purposes:
1. An application;
2. The protocol of the founders' meeting or, if the LLC has only one founder, the resolution of the founder on the establishment of the LLC;
3. The charter of the LLC;
4. A copy of the passport of the proposed general director of the LLC;
5. Power(s) of attorney issued by the founder(s) for establishment of the LLC;
6. Power(s) of attorney issued by the founder(s) for filing the application for the state registration of the LLC;
7. Confirmation of the legal status of the founder(s) (e.g., extract from the trade register or certificate of good standing);
8. The charter (articles of association, by-laws) of foreign legal entities;
9. Confirmation of payment of the state registration fee;

10. Foreign tax registration certificate of the founders (to be provided to a bank);
11. Bank letter of good credit standing of a foreign legal entity; and
12. Confirmation of the foreign legal entity's contribution to the charter capital of the LLC.

Any Russian founder participating in an LLC must also provide additional documentation. All documents from a foreign legal entity must be notarized and apostilled/legalized in the country of preparation. Any document supplied in a language other than Russian must be accompanied by a Russian translation which has a notarized certification.

Chapter 13: Joint Stock Companies in Russia

Types of Joint Stock Companies

A significant number of commercial organizations have been established since the JSC Law came into force on 1 January 1996. While the adoption of the LLC Law in 1998 introduced another option for investors seeking to establish a corporate entity, the JSC Law represents one of the most significant pieces of civil legislation of the post-Soviet era; JSCs remain among the most common commercial corporate forms and structures for doing business in Russia.

A JSC is a legal entity which issues shares in order to raise capital for its activities. A shareholder of a JSC is not generally liable for the obligations of the JSC and bears the risk of any loss only in the amount paid by it for the shares.

Two types of joint stock companies exist in Russia:
1. Closed joint stock companies; and
2. Open joint stock companies.

An open JSC may have an unlimited number of shareholders. Shareholders in an open JSC are entitled to freely dispose of their shares.

The number of shareholders in a closed JSC may not exceed 50, and the JSC must be transformed into an open JSC within one year should this number be exceeded. As with participants in an LLC, shareholders in a closed JSC have a right of first refusal to acquire shares sold by other shareholders to third parties, at the price offered to the third parties.

Shareholders in both open and closed JSCs have a pre-emptive right to acquire newly issued shares that are to be privately placed, in proportion to their existing shareholdings. Shareholders in an open JSC also have a pre-emptive right to acquire newly issued shares that are to be publicly placed, in proportion to their existing shareholdings, but do not have a right of first refusal to acquire shares sold by another shareholder to third parties.

All JSCs are required to maintain a shareholder register. The register includes information about each registered shareholder including the number, category, and classes of shares held. A JSC with more than 500 shareholders must delegate the keeping of the shareholder register to a licensed registrar.

Formation of a Joint Stock Company

Individuals and legal entities may be the founders of a JSC. A company's foundation document, i.e., its charter, must include the following information:

1. The name, address, and type of the JSC (i.e., open or closed);
2. The size of the JSC charter capital;
3. The quantity, nominal value, and categories (common or preferred) of shares, as well as the classes of preferred shares issued and distributed by the JSC;

4. The rights of the holders of shares of each category;
5. The structure and competence of the governing bodies of the JSC, and their decision-making procedures;
6. The procedure for preparing for and holding general meetings of shareholders, including a list of issues requiring either unanimous consent or a resolution adopted by a qualified majority of votes;
7. Information on branches and representative offices;
8. Information on the existence of any special right of participation in the management of the company (a "golden share") held by the Russian Federation, a constituent entity of the Russian Federation, or a municipality of the Russian Federation; and
9. Other provisions required by law.

The charter may include other provisions, so long as these comply with applicable Russian legislation.

Charter Capital

The charter capital of an open JSC may not be less than 1,000 times the Russian statutory monthly minimum wage (the monthly minimum wage used for the purposes of calculating the minimum charter capital of the JSC is currently RUB100). Currently, using an exchange rate of approximately 30 RUB/USD, the minimum charter capital for an open JSC is approx. USD3,333. A closed joint stock company must have a minimum charter capital equivalent to at least 100 times the minimum monthly wage (i.e. the minimum capital is currently approx. USD333).

In contrast to LLC founders, the founders of a JSC must pay 50% of the JSC charter capital within three months following its state registration, with the balance payable in full within the first year.

Shares and Other Types of Securities

A JSC can issue securities in the form of shares, bonds, and issuer's options. Such securities must be registered with the Federal Service for the Financial Markets of the Russian Federation (the "FSFM"), which replaced the former Federal Commission for the Securities Market (the "FCSM") in March 2004. A JSC can issue common shares and/or several classes of preferred shares. The total value of a JSC's preferred shares may not exceed 25% of its charter capital.

The concept of a "fractional share" was introduced on 1 January 2002. A fractional share is a share representing a portion of a whole share, which can come into existence when it is not possible to acquire the whole share during a consolidation of shares, when a shareholder exercises its pre-emptive right, or in the course of acquiring newly issued shares. A fractional share grants its owner the same rights that are granted by the whole share of the corresponding category or class, on a pro rata basis.

Management Structure

Both open and closed JSCs must maintain two governing bodies: the general meeting of shareholders and the executive body. An open JSC with more than 50 shareholders must also have a board of directors (also called a supervisory board). An open JSC with less than 50 shareholders and all closed JSCs may appoint a board of directors, although this is not a requirement. The authority of the board of directors is defined by the charter of the JSC and, if a board is not provided for in the charter, the corresponding authority is held by the JSC's general meeting of shareholders.

In addition to the foregoing governing bodies, a JSC must either establish an internal auditing commission or elect an internal auditor to oversee its financial and economic activities, members of which must be elected by the shareholders.

The general meeting of shareholders is the highest governing body overseeing the activities of a JSC. Its authority is outlined in the JSC Law and cannot be altered. Each common share carries one vote at the general meeting of shareholders (except for cases of cumulative voting where provided for in the JSC Law), and most decisions are made by a simple majority vote, although for certain key decisions a supermajority of 75% is required.

The daily management of a JSC is the responsibility of the executive body, which may be one person the general director or may consist of both the general director and the management council. The executive body is responsible for all matters that do not fall within the authority of either the board of directors or the general meeting of shareholders. The general meeting may (by a majority vote) choose to delegate the powers of the executive body to an external commercial organization or to an individual manager on a contractual basis; however this decision may be taken only pursuant to a proposal from the board of directors (if the company has a board of directors).

Chapter 14: Competition Protection Law in Russia

Antitrust matters in Russia are regulated by the Federal Law on Protection of Competition (the "Competition Law") effective as of 26 October 2006 (as last amended on 6 December 2011) and fall under the auspices of the Federal Antimonopoly Service ("FAS").

The Competition Law has extra-territorial effect. This means that its provisions extend to relations (agreements, actions) that arise (are concluded, performed) among and by Russian and/or non-Russian persons in and/or outside of Russia, and that affect (or may affect) competition in the Russian Federation.

The Competition Law regulates competition in both the commodities market and financial services markets, and includes the following main areas of particular interest to foreign investors:
1. Abuse of a dominant position;
2. Agreements and concerted actions limiting competition;
3. State preferences;
4. Establishment of companies;
5. Mergers and acquisitions;
6. Unfair competition;
7. Requirements for tenders and quotation requests.

Abuse of a Dominant Position

Dominant entities are subject to certain restrictions on their activities. Determining whether a particular entity enjoys a dominant position involves a complex evaluation of various factors, the most important of which is the entity's market share.

For entities with a market share of 50% or greater there is a presumption of market dominance. Entities with a market share of between 35% and 50% are deemed dominant, provided their dominant position has been established by the FAS.

For entities with a market share of 35% or less there is a presumption of non-dominance, with a few exceptions provided by the Competition Law. Namely, an entity with a market share of less than 35% can be deemed to hold a dominant position if it has a decisive influence on the conditions of product circulation in the market.

The FAS deems a financial organization to be a dominant entity according to the criteria/thresholds set by the Russian Government (and with respect to credit organizations, together with the Russian Central Bank). A financial organization whose share in any single market in the Russian Federation does not exceed 10%, or whose share does not exceed 20% in a commodity market if the commodity also circulates in other commodity markets in the Russian Federation, may not be deemed dominant.

When determining market share, the FAS may take into account not merely one company in isolation but also the group of companies to which it belongs. The group will include all persons/legal entities related by a common controlling share ownership, contractual or other actually in management control.

In addition to the term "dominant position" the Competition Law has a concept of "collective dominant position", i.e. the collective domination of the market by between three and five independent companies. According to the Competition Law, a participant in collective domination can hold as little as 8% of the market for a certain commodity and be viewed as a violator if it, together with one or two other participants, has more than 50% of the given market, or, together with up to four other participants, holds more than 70% of the market, and such entities meet certain criteria specified in the Competition Law.

For those in a dominant position, the Competition Law prohibits any of the following activities:
1. Setting and/or maintaining monopolistically high or low prices;
2. Withdrawal of goods from circulation if the result of such a withdrawal is a rise of the price of the goods;
3. Creation of conditions that place one or more business entities in an unequal position as compared to other entities in their ability to access the market for particular goods (creation of discriminatory conditions);

4. Imposition of contractual terms that are disadvantageous to the other party or do not relate to the subject matter of the contract (and which are not economically or technologically justified);
5. Discontinuance or reduction of production of goods for which there is a consumer demand if it is possible to produce them on a profitable basis;
6. Unjustified refusal to enter into a contract with particular customers if it is possible to provide the relevant goods to such customers;
7. Setting different prices for the same goods where this is not economically or technologically justified;
8. Creation of barriers to market entry or exit for other business entities;
9. Violation of pricing rules established by legislation;
10. Price gouging in the wholesale and (or) retail electricity markets.

Some of the above activities may be allowed if the dominant entity can prove that the positive effects of a particular activity outweigh its negative consequences pursuant to the criteria set in the Competition Law.

Agreements, Concerted Actions and Actions of State Bodies Limiting Competition

Agreements Limiting Competition

The Competition Law prohibits cartels, i.e. agreements concluded between competitors acting on the same market, if such agreements lead or may lead to the following:

1. Control or fixing of prices, discounts, bonus payments, or surcharges;
2. Increase or reduction of prices or the manipulation of prices at tenders;
3. Division of the market by territory or according to the volume of sales/purchases, the range of marketable goods, or the range of sellers or buyers;
4. Refusal to deal with particular sellers or customers;
5. Discontinuance or reduction of production of goods.

The Competition Law prohibits vertical agreements (i.e. agreements between firms at different levels of the supply chain) if they

1. Lead to resale price fixing, save for fixing of a maximum resale price, and/or
2. Impose an obligation on the buyer not to permit the sale of a competitor's products unless the sales are arranged by the buyer under the trademark or other means of individualization of the respective manufacturer or supplier.

The Competition Law prohibits agreements between economic entities acting on wholesale and (or) retail electricity markets and commercial or technological infrastructure markets if such agreements lead to price gouging on the wholesale and (or) retail electricity markets.

The Competition Law further prohibits other agreements that lead or may lead to restriction of competition. Such agreements might impose unfavourable conditions on the counterparty, set different prices for the same goods without economic or technologic justification, create barriers for third parties entering into or exiting from a certain market, establish conditions for participating in professional or other communities.

In addition, the Competition Law prohibits the so-called "coordination of economic activities" by economic entities if such coordination may lead to restriction of competition. "Coordination of economic activities" is understood as coordination of the actions of economic entities by a third person who does not belong to the "group of persons" of such economic entities and does not act on the market where coordination is taking place. Pursuant to the Competition Law, any actions under and within a vertical agreement are not treated as the coordination of economic activities.

At the same time the Competition Law provides certain exemptions from the above restrictions, in particular.

1. Except for cartels, the Competition Law permits vertical agreements that are concluded between economic entities each having a market share of less than 20% in any market;

and/or that are commercial concession (franchise) agreements concluded in written form.

2. Save for cartels, an agreement may be recognized as permissible if it can be proved that such agreement does not lead to elimination of competition, does not impose excessive restrictions on the parties to it or third parties and the positive effects of the agreement, including socio-economic effects, outweigh its negative consequences pursuant to the criteria set in the Competition Law.

3. An agreement on joint activities, even if it leads to the consequences of a cartel arrangement, may be recognized as permissible if it can be proved that such agreement does not lead to elimination of competition, does not impose any restrictions on third parties and the positive effects of the agreement, including socio-economic effects, outweigh its negative consequences pursuant to the criteria set in the Competition Law.

4. Agreements entered into between companies of the same group of persons, if either party to the agreement controls, is controlled by or is under common control with the other party to the agreement are exempt from all the restrictions. Control for this purpose is understood as the ability of one person or entity to determine directly or indirectly the decisions taken by the other entity either

through use of more than 50% of voting shares in, or by performing the functions of an executive body of, such entity.

5. Agreements on provision or disposal of the right to use the results of intellectual activity or means of individualization are exempt from all the restrictions.

In addition the Russian Government has introduced general exemptions in a number of economic areas providing certain rules and criteria for recognizing the agreements in such areas as permissible.

Concerted Actions Limiting Competition

The Competition Law prohibits concerted actions made by competitors acting on the same market, if such concerted actions lead to the following:

1. Control or fixing of prices, discounts, bonus payments, or surcharges.
2. Increase or reduction of prices or the manipulation of prices at tenders.
3. Division of the market by territory or according to the volume of sales/purchases, the range of marketable goods, or the range of sellers or buyers.
4. Refusal to deal with particular sellers or customers unless such refusal is envisaged by federal legislation.
5. Discontinuance or reduction of production of goods.

Under the Competition Law "concerted actions" are understood as actions carried out by economic entities without agreement, if such actions meet the following criteria:

1. The outcome of such actions is in the interest of each of the participating economic entities.
2. Each economic entity is aware of such actions due to a public announcement made by one of the economic entities participating in the concerted actions.
3. The actions of each of the economic entities are based on the actions of other economic entities and do not result from circumstances equally affecting all economic entities in the market.

In addition, the Competition Law prohibits concerted actions made by economic entities acting on the wholesale and (or) retail electricity markets and commercial or technological infrastructure markets if such agreements lead to price gouging on the wholesale and (or) retail electricity markets.

The Competition Law further prohibits other concerted actions that lead to restriction of competition, including concerted actions that create unfavourable conditions for a counterparty, the setting of different prices for the same goods without economic or technologic justification, creating barriers for third parties trying to enter into or exit from a certain market.

In certain cases some concerted actions may be permitted if it can be proved that the positive effects of the actions, including socioeconomic effects, outweigh their negative consequences pursuant to the criteria set in the Competition Law.

The above-mentioned prohibitions are not applied to the concerted actions made
1. By persons whose aggregate market share does not exceed 20% and the share of each of them does not exceed 8%, or
2. Among the same group of persons if one of the participants controls or is under common control with the other participant of concerted actions.

Acts and Actions of State Bodies Limiting Competition

The Competition Law also provides certain restrictions applicable to the acts, actions, omissions, agreements and concerted actions of federal executive state bodies, the Central Bank, non-budgetary funds, regional and municipal state bodies and organizations performing state functions or providing state services that may lead to the limiting, restricting or eliminating of competition.

In particular, actions that results in:
1. Introducing restrictions when establishing legal entities,
2. Establishing prohibitions on the movement of goods within Russia or other restrictions on the sale, purchase or exchange of goods,
3. Limiting the right to choose suppliers,

4. Granting state preferences in breach of prescribed procedure,
5. Creation of discriminatory conditions and some others actions are prohibited by the Competition Law.

State Preferences

State and municipal preferences were introduced by the Competition Law in 2006. In accordance with the Competition Law, state (or municipal) preferences consist of granting an economic entity certain privileges over other market participants, ensuring more favourable conditions for its activity in the relevant market by transferring property and (or) civil rights, preferences or state (or municipal) guarantees.

The Competition Law regulates the procedure for providing state (or municipal) preferences for the following purposes:
1. Ensuring vital services for the population in Arctic regions and equivalent areas.
2. Development of science and education.
3. Carrying out fundamental scientific research.
4. Environmental protection.
5. Cultural development and conservation of the cultural heritage.
6. Development of sports and physical culture.
7. Agricultural production.
8. State defence and security;
9. Rendering social services to the population.
10. Health and labour protection.
11. Rendering support to small or medium businesses, etc.

State (or municipal) preferences shall be granted with the preliminary written approval of the FAS, subject to a few exceptions specified in the Competition Law.

In order to provide state (or municipal) preferences, the authority intending to grant the preferences submits an application to the FAS for approval together with supporting documents (including a draft act providing for the granting of the state (or municipal) preferences with an indication of the goals and amounts of the preferences; a list of the beneficiary's activities over the two years preceding the date of the FAS application; and other information required by the Competition Law).

The FAS takes a decision on the application within one month from the moment it is submitted together with all necessary documents. The FAS may extend the period for review of the application by up to two months if the FAS believes that granting such state (or municipal) preferences may lead to restriction of competition.

Chapter 15: Mergers and Acquisitions in Russia

Acquisitions

The Competition Law stipulates that the following transactions and other actions are subject to state control if certain thresholds are met:

1. Transactions with the assets of Russian financial organizations.
2. Transactions with main production (fixed) assets and (or) intangible assets which are located in Russia.
3. Transactions with voting shares, participatory interests or rights in Russian commercial and non-commercial legal entities.
4. Transactions with voting shares, participatory interests or rights in foreign companies supplying goods to the Russian Federation worth more than RUB1 billion (approx. USD33.3 million) during the year preceding the transaction.

Establishment of Companies

The founders must obtain consent from (FAS) Federal Antimonopoly Service prior to the establishment of a new company (be it Russian or foreign) provided its charter capital is paid in-kind with the shares and/or property of a Russian legal entity and the new company acquires (as payment of its charter capital) more than 25%/50%/75% of such shares or more than ⅓ /50% / ⅔ of such participatory shares, or where the company acquires more 20% of the main production (fixed) assets and (or) intangible assets located in Russia (exclusive of most types of buildings and land plots) of another legal entity, and where the thresholds set in the Competition Law are met.

According to specific conditions provided by the Competition Law, the establishment of a company whose charter capital is paid using the shares and/or property of a Russian financial organization may be subject to mandatory FAS notification prior to establishment. These conditions are similar to those described above for entities acting in the commodities market with certain differences that should be considered on a case-by-case basis.

Mergers

The consolidation or merger of legal entities (save for financial organizations) is subject to the prior approval of the FAS if the aggregate asset value of these entities and their group of persons exceeds RUB7 billion (approx. USD233.3 million) or the aggregate revenue earned by the entities and their "group of persons" from the sale of goods during the past calendar year exceeds RUB10 billion (approx. USD333.3 million) or if either of the entities is included in the FAS register of entities with a market share exceeding 35% in the relevant market. The procedures for obtaining such approval are similar to the procedures used for acquisitions.

As for the consolidations or mergers involving financial organizations, the respective thresholds are set depending on the type of financial organizations involved by the Russian Government.

Intra-group consolidations or mergers may be exempt from the requirement to obtain prior FAS approval, provided certain conditions are met.

Acquisition of an Interest, Assets and Rights in a Russian Company Acquisition of Shares/Participatory Interest in a Russian Company When an individual, legal entity or group of persons acquires more than 25%/50%/75% of voting shares or more than ⅓ / 50% / ⅔ of participatory shares in a Russian entity, such persons, entities or group must receive prior approval from FAS if:

1. The aggregate book value of the assets of the acquirer and its "group of persons" plus the target and its "group of persons" exceeds RUB7 billion (approx. USD233.3 million) and the balance sheet value of the total assets of the target and its group exceeds RUB250 million (approx. USD8.3 million); or

2. The aggregate revenue earned by the acquirer and its "group of persons" plus the target and its "group of persons" from the sale of goods over the past calendar year exceeds RUB10 billion (approx. USD333.3 million) and the balance sheet value of the total assets of the target and its group exceeds RUB250 million (approx. USD8.3 million); or

3. Either the acquirer, or any of the entities belonging to its "group of persons", or the

target, or any of the entities belonging to its "group of persons", is included in the FAS register of entities with a market share exceeding 35% in the relevant market.

Acquisition of Assets Located in Russia

When an individual, legal entity or group of persons acquires the right of ownership or the right to use the main production (fixed) assets located in Russia or intangible assets of a Russian or foreign entity (subject to certain exceptions provided in the Competition Law), if the acquired assets account for more than 20% of the aggregate book value of the main production (fixed) assets and intangible assets of the selling entity, such persons, entities or a group of entities involved in the acquisition must receive prior approval from FAS if:

1. The aggregate book value of the assets of the acquirer and its "group of persons" plus the target and its "group of persons" exceeds RUB7 billion (approx. USD233.3 million) and the balance sheet value of the total assets of the target and its group exceeds RUB250 million (approx. USD8.3 million); or

2. The aggregate revenue earned by the acquirer and its "group of persons" plus the target and its "group of persons" from the sale of goods during the past calendar year exceeds RUB10 billion (approx. USD333.3 million) and the balance sheet value of the total assets of the target and its group exceeds RUB250 million (approx. USD8.3 million); or

3. Either the acquirer, or any of the entities belonging to its "group of persons", or the target, or any of the entities belonging to its "group of persons", is included in the FAS register of entities with a market share exceeding 35% in the relevant market.

The main production (fixed) assets or intangible assets of an entity to be transferred taken into account for the purposes of the above calculation do not include land plots and non-industrial buildings, constructions, premises and parts thereof or unfinished construction objects.

Acquisition of Rights in a Russian Company

When an individual, legal entity or group of persons acquires rights conferring the ability to determine the commercial behaviour of the target company (including as a result of change of indirect control over a Russian target company) or the right to perform the functions of its executive bodies, such persons, entities or group must receive prior approval from FAS if:
1. The aggregate book value of the assets of the acquirer and its "group of persons" plus the target and its "group of persons" exceeds RUB7 billion (approx. USD233.3 million) and the balance sheet value of the total assets of the target and its group exceeds RUB250 million (approx. USD8.3 million); or
2. The aggregate revenue earned by the acquirer and its "group of persons" plus the target and its "group of persons" from the sale of goods

over the past calendar year exceeds RUB10 billion (approx. USD333.3 million) and the balance sheet value of the total assets of the target and its group exceeds RUB250 million (approx. USD8.3 million); or

3. Either the acquirer, or any of the entities belonging to its "group of persons", or the target, or any of the entities belonging to its "group of persons", is included in the FAS register of entities with a market share exceeding 35% in the relevant market.

Mergers and acquisitions outside of Russia which require Russian anti-trust approval when an individual, legal entity or group of persons acquires more than 50% of the voting shares of, or any right of control over, a legal entity incorporated outside Russia, or the right to perform the functions of its executive bodies, the acquirer must receive prior approval from FAS if:

1. Such target foreign legal entity controls a Russian subsidiary, or such target foreign legal entity supplied goods to the Russian Federation worth more than RUB1 billion (approx. USD33.3 million) during the year preceding the transaction; and

2. The aggregate book value of the assets of the acquirer and its "group of persons" plus the target and its "group of persons" exceeds RUB7 billion (approx. USD233.3 million) and the balance sheet value of the total assets of the target and its group exceeds RUB250 million (approx. USD8.3 million); or

3. The aggregate revenue earned by the acquirer and its "group of persons" plus the target and its "group of persons" from the sale of goods over the past calendar year exceeds RUB10 billion (approx. USD333.3 million) and the balance sheet value of the total assets of the target and its group exceeds RUB250 million (approx. USD8.3 million); or

4. Either the acquirer, or any of the entities belonging to its "group of persons", or the target, or any of the entities belonging to its "group of persons", is included in the FAS register of entities with a market share exceeding 35% in the relevant market.

If any of the thresholds established for consolidations, mergers or acquisitions of voting shares, participatory interest, assets or rights described above is not met and due to this fact the prior approval of FAS is not required, FAS still must be notified within 45 days post closing if:

1. The aggregate book value of the assets or the aggregate revenue earned by the consolidated or merged companies exceeds RUB400 million (approx. USD13.3 million); or

2. The aggregate book value of the assets or the aggregate revenue earned by the acquirer and its "group of persons" plus the target and its "group of persons" exceeds RUB400 million (approx. USD13.3 million) and the balance sheet value of the total assets of the target and its "group of persons" exceeds RUB60 million (approx. USD2 million).

The Russian Government establishes other thresholds for the notification requirement for financial organizations which are involved in such transactions.

In determining the threshold for asset and revenue values, FAS takes into consideration not only the acquirer and the target company, but also all persons (individuals or legal entities) in the acquirer's and target's "group of persons." The broad term "group of persons" includes all individuals or legal entities related to the acquirer/target as a result of controlling share ownership or through certain management contracts, familial relations, and/or other de facto control mechanisms.

This term, however, does not include the seller of the shares in question and its group of persons provided, as a result of the transaction, the seller/its group loses the controlling right.

Where a merger or acquisition takes place between entities in the same "group of persons" and preliminary approval by FAS would normally be required by law, the Competition Law permits post transaction notification of FAS within 45 days after the transaction is completed instead of preliminary approval, provided that the transaction is made between a parent company and its direct subsidiary. In other cases the Competition Law permits post transaction notification of FAS within 45 days after the transaction is completed, provided the group structure is submitted to FAS no later than one month prior to the transaction and the group structure does not change until after the transaction is completed.

The Competition Law contains separate articles for the acquisitions of an interest, assets and/or rights in financial organizations that are subject to pre-acquisition FAS notification, and the articles contain specific conditions and thresholds applicable to such acquisitions that should be considered on a case-by-case basis.

Procedures and Timing

If FAS determines that an establishment of a company or a merger, or acquisition may restrict competition or strengthen a dominant position it may request additional information and documentation. FAS may also require the parties to take measures to ensure competition.

After all documents have been submitted, FAS has 30 days to review the application or notification. If FAS believes that the transaction may lead to restriction of competition, the review period may be prolonged for an additional two months, during which FAS places information about the transaction on its official web-site and invites all interested parties to voice their opinions on the transaction.

Unfair Competition

Unfair competition, namely any actions by commercial entities aimed at acquiring a competitive advantage in commercial activity in contravention of the Competition Law, business customs, the requirements of good-faith, reasonableness and fairness, which may or have caused losses to other competing legal entities, or damage their business reputation, is prohibited in Russia.

Types of activities that constitute unfair competition include:
1. Distribution of false, inaccurate or distorted information that may cause losses to a commercial entity or damage this entity's business reputation.
2. Misleading consumers about the nature, methods and place of production, as well as consumer properties and quality, of goods;
3. Incorrect comparison by a commercial entity of goods produced or sold by this entity with the goods of other commercial entities.
4. Sale of goods with the illegal use of the results of intellectual activity (i.e., intellectual property) and of the means of individualization of a commercial entity, products, or services, such as trademarks, logotypes and other objects of intellectual property.
5. Receipt, use and disclosure of commercial, official or other secrets, without the consent of the commercial entity to which this information belongs, etc.

Requirements for Tenders and Price Quotations

The Competition Law provides a list of actions in conducting tenders and requesting price quotations (including governmental tenders) which are prohibited if they lead to a restriction of competition (for example, the creation of preferential conditions for participation in tenders, violation of the procedure for determining the winner, etc).

All federal and municipal bodies, bodies of the Russian Federation's constituent entities and non-budgetary funds must select a financial organization by holding a public tender (in line with the procedures set by other federal laws) to render certain financial services, a full list of which is provided by the Competition Law, and which includes rendering services on the securities market, attracting monetary funds from legal entities, opening and maintaining bank accounts for legal entities, and making settlements with these accounts, etc.

The Competition Law provides a procedure for referring disputes relating to violations of tender procedures to FAS. This mechanism is additional and without prejudice to the possibility of challenging tender results in Russian courts.

Chapter 16: Russia Accession to the World Trade Organisation

On 16 December 2011 Russia was officially approved to join the WTO. Russia's commitments and obligations are established in the Protocol of Accession of Russia to the WTO dated 16 December 2011 (hereinafter – the "WTO Accession Protocol") and the Working Party Report on the Accession of Russia to the WTO dated 17 November 2011 are publicly available. In order to become a member state of the WTO, Russia should ratify the WTO Accession Protocol by the end of August 2012.

Market access for goods, tariff and quota commitments

On average the final legally binding tariff ceiling for the Russian Federation will be 7.8% compared with a 2011 average of 10% for all products:

1. The average tariff ceiling for agriculture products will be 10.8% lower than the current average of 13.2%.
2. The ceiling average for manufactured goods will be 7.3% vs. the 9.5% average today on manufactured imports.

Russia has agreed to lower its tariffs on a wide range of products. Average duties after full implementation of tariff reductions will be:

1. 14.9% for dairy products (current tariff 19.8%).

2. 10.0% for cereals (current tariff 15.1%).
3. 7.1% for oilseeds, fats and oils (current tariff 9.0%).
4. 5.2% for chemicals (current tariff 6.5%).
5. 12.0% for automobiles (current tariff 15.5%).
6. 6.2% for electrical machinery (current tariff 8.4%).
7. 8.0% for wood and paper (current tariff 13.4%).
8. USD223 per ton for sugar (current tariff USD243 per ton).

Tariffs will be bound at zero for cotton and information technology (ITA) products (the current tariff on ITA products is 5.4%).

It should be noted, however, that 90% of the initial rates of import duties that should be applied from the date of accession to the WTO, as set out in the WTO Accession Protocol, are higher than the rates of the Common Tariff of the Customs Union that was applied before the date of accession. This means that Russia retains the right to increase import duty rates for certain types of goods, which is unlikely at the moment.

The final bound rate will be implemented on the date of accession for more than one third of the national tariff lines with another quarter of the tariff cuts to be put in place during a transition period of 3-7 years provided for each particular good.

The longest implementation period is eight years for poultry, followed by seven years for motor cars, helicopters and civil aircraft.

Tariff rate quotas (TRQs) will be applied to beef, pork and poultry products. Imports entering the market within the quota will face lower tariffs while higher duties will be applied to products imported outside the quota.

The in-quota and out-of-quota rates are listed below with the out-of quota rates in parentheses:
1. For beef 15% (duty rate out of quota 55%).
2. For pork zero (duty rate out of quota 65%). The TRQ for pork will be replaced by a flat top rate of 25% as of 1 January 2020; 25% (duty rate out of quota 80%) for some selected poultry products.
3. Some of these quotas are also subject to member-specific allocations.

Export duties

Export duties will be binding for over 700 tariff lines, including certain fish and crustaceans, mineral fuels and oils, raw hides and skins, wood, pulp and paper, and base metal products.

Market access for services

Russia made market access commitments in 11 services sectors and 116 sub-sectors. No market access restrictions were provided for 30 sectors, including advertising, market research, consulting and management services. At the same time, Russia did not make any commitments for 39 sectors, including pipeline, railroad and internal water transport, medical services and scientific research activities, i.e., market access for foreign companies would still be restricted in these areas.

Russia maintained certain limitations on market access and national treatment with respect to various types of services that are provided in the Russia's WTO Accession Protocol. For example, priority is provided for Russian entities acting as contractors, suppliers and carriers that participate in production sharing agreements for exploration, development and production of mineral raw materials.

Foreign insurance companies would be allowed to establish Russian branches 9 years after Russia joins the WTO, i.e., in 2012.

Foreign banks would be allowed to establish subsidiaries in Russia. There would be no cap on foreign equity in individual banking institutions, but the overall foreign capital participation in the banking system of the Russian Federation would be limited to 50% (not including foreign capital invested in potentially privatized banks).

On distribution services, Russia would allow 100% foreign-owned companies to engage in wholesale, retail and franchise sectors upon accession to the WTO.

Other commitments

Russia made a commitment to gradually decrease domestic support for agricultural sector from USD9 billion in 2012 to USD4.4 billion by 2018.

Russia has maintained the right to impose strict limitations on market access and national treatment for foreign persons in such sectors as energy, telecommunications and education. On telecommunications, the foreign equity limitation (49%) would be eliminated during the four years following accession. The Russian Federation also agreed to apply the terms of the WTO's Basic Telecommunications Agreement.

Chapter 17: Customs Union

Since the formation of the CU (custom union) the territories of Russia, Belarus and Kazakhstan comprise a unified customs territory. The CU has unified rules for foreign trade activity, including the importation and exportation of goods. Once goods are imported and released in any CU member state such goods may be freely moved within the CU.

There is no customs clearance or customs control at the internal state border between Russia and Belarus and between Russia and Kazakhstan.

The supreme authority of the CU is the Intergovernmental Counsel of EurAsEC. The Commission of the CU is a supranational regulatory and executive body of the CU that is authorized to take implementing regulations and monitor execution of the regulations of the CU by its member states.

The CU is a stage in the formation of the Unified Economic Area, which is expected to imply free movement of services, workforce, and capital within the unified territory. The basic agreements on the formation of the Unified Economic Area have already been signed by Russia, Belarus and Kazakhstan (on unified macroeconomic policy, market access for various sectors, etc.) and are expected to take effect in 2012. It is expected that the Unified Economic Area will be established gradually by 2020 for most economic sectors, such as; free trade in services, including market access to natural monopolies (e.g., railways, energy, etc.); access to financial services, including free movement of capital; a unified social policy and free movement of workforce; unified competition laws; a concerted macroeconomic policy, etc.

Unified Tariff Regulation of the Customs Union

The classification of goods for customs purposes in Russia is carried out in accordance with the Unified Customs Tariff of the CU, which is based on the International Convention on the Harmonized Commodity Description and Coding System, dated 14 June 1983 (the Harmonized System), providing that all the goods crossing the customs territory of the CU are assigned customs classification codes (HS codes) determined in accordance with the general rules of interpretation of the Harmonized System. Customs authorities control the correctness
of the classification of goods.

Preliminary Classification Decisions

At the discretion of importers of record, the Russian customs authorities may take preliminary decisions on classification of goods (hereinafter – "a preliminary classification decision") which is equivalent to binding tariff information used in the USA and the EU.

Information and documents provided by applicants for the preliminary classification (such as technical descriptions, pictures, samples, etc.) should be exhaustive and should contain all the data required for proper determination of a HS classification code.

Preliminary classification decisions are issued in the name of the applicants (i.e., importers of record) and may only be used by them.

The timing for issuance of a preliminary classification decision is 90 calendar days from the date of filing an application, which may be extended for a number of reasons provided by law.

Preliminary classification decisions are valid for three years and are mandatory for all Russian customs authorities with respect to the classified goods.

Sanitary-Epidemiologic Measures

Unified sanitary measures of the CU are applied in order to confirm that goods imported and distributed in CU territory comply with all safety requirements and do not pose any threat to life and health. The unified sanitary rules are applied at the external border and within the whole territory of the CU and include three lists of goods:

1. The list of goods that are subject to sanitary-epidemiologic control (includes almost all food products and consumer goods). Goods falling under this list must comply with the established sanitary and safety requirements;

2. The list of goods that are subject to state registration, which is required in order to confirm compliance with sanitary epidemiologic and hygiene requirements and applies to food products, cosmetic and household chemical products, certain clothing items, mineral water, alcoholic beverages, etc.

The state registration must be carried out prior to the goods' importation into the CU;

3. The list of exemptions from state registration (for example, when goods subject to state registration are imported for exhibition purposes).

Technical Regulation (Confirmation of Compliance)

Confirmation of compliance is designed to confirm that goods conform to the statutory quality and consumer characteristics requirements. Confirmation of compliance in Russia is based on the Russian national regulations and on the legislation of the CU and the EurAsEC.

The technical rules of the CU establish a unified list of goods that are subject to mandatory confirmation of compliance in the form of (i) certification or (ii) declaration of compliance, as well as unified forms for the (i) certificate and (ii) declaration of compliance that are issued by the accredited agencies and laboratories of the CU member states and are valid throughout the CU. It should be noted that compliance confirmation of foreign goods imported into Russia may be performed with certification only.

The technical rules of the CU envisage adoption of a number of technical regulations with requirements for goods on the aforementioned unified list, including 47 priority CU technical regulations. As of December 2011, about 24 technical regulations were adopted (e.g., on the safety of perfumes and cosmetics;

packaging; toys, grain, vehicles, machinery, foodstuff, juices, fat-and oil products, etc.). It is expected that the majority of technical regulations will be adopted by 31 December 2012. Once the CU or EurAsEC technical regulations come into force they would be applied with direct effect and relevant Russian national requirements should no longer be applied. It is expected that by 31 December 2014 all national mandatory technical requirements would be replaced by the CU technical regulations or would no longer be applied. The EurAsEC technical regulations would duplicate CU technical regulations.

It should be noted that currently the technical rules of the CU are still being formed and currently national standards and national lists of products that are subject to mandatory confirmation of compliance also still exist separately in Russia, Belarus and Kazakhstan.

Therefore, currently the two different systems of compliance confirmation co-exist in the CU, i.e., the unified system of the CU and separately applied national (local) technical rules of Russia, Belarus and Kazakhstan. Prior to importation of goods into any of the CU member states it is important to ensure that the goods are in compliance with both systems of compliance confirmation.

In order to facilitate and improve the Russian system of technical regulation a Federal Service on Accreditation was established at the end of 2011, which should be a common body responsible for the accreditation of certification bodies and testing laboratories, maintenance of registers and state supervision.

Phytosanitary and Veterinary Control

Importation into Russia of certain types of products, such as living animals, animal foods, meat, meat products, seafood, plants, etc. are subject to special supervision (control) in accordance with the unified veterinary and phytosanitary rules of the CU. Thus, a consignment with controllable goods can be imported into Russia in accordance with the unified veterinary requirements of the CU and with special permission (a veterinary or phytosanitary certificate) issued in the established procedure by the Russian Federal Service on Veterinary and Phytosanitary Supervision (Rosselhoznadzor), which is responsible for monitoring controllable goods and maintaining the register of foreign companies authorized to export certain goods into Russia, as well as lists of certain products banned for importation into Russia from third countries.

Chapter 18: Employment in Russia

The principal legislation governing labour relationships in the Russian Federation is the Labour Code of the Russian Federation (the "Labour Code"), effective 1 February 2002, as amended through 2011. In addition to this core legislation, labour relationships are regulated by the 1996 Federal Law On Trade Unions, Their Rights and Guarantees of Activity, as amended (currently through 2011), as well as Russian legislation on minimum wages, labour safety and other related laws and numerous regulations.

Russian labour law applies equally to regular employees and top managers, including the CEOs of Russian companies and heads of representative offices and branch offices of foreign companies accredited in Russia. Russian labour law also applies to foreign nationals employed by Russian or foreign businesses in Russia. All employers should comply with special immigration law requirements for foreign employees.

A written employment agreement in Russian setting out the basic terms and conditions of the employment relationship must be entered into with each employee working in Russia. The Labour Code provides all employees with mandatory minimum guarantees and employment-related benefits and compensations, which cannot be superseded by the agreement between the employer and the employee.

Accordingly, any provisions in an employment agreement that impair the employee's position as compared to that set forth by such guarantees will be invalid. As a general rule employment agreements are entered into for an indefinite period of time. A definite term (fixed-term) employment agreement may also be concluded, but such an agreement cannot be enforced for longer than five years, and it may only be concluded when the nature or conditions of work make it impossible for the parties to enter into an indefinite term agreement, in particular in the circumstances specifically provided for by Article 59 of the Labour Code. Further, an employee cannot be prohibited from holding a second job in addition to his/her full-time employment, with certain limited exceptions and restrictions provided by the Labour Code and other federal laws.

Under Russian labour legislation the relevant employment duties and obligations must be expressly defined in the employment agreement. It is important that these duties and obligations are defined broadly enough since an employee cannot be required to perform tasks outside the scope of job duties expressly described in his/her employment agreement.

The employer cannot expand or otherwise modify them unilaterally without the written consent of the employee. Similarly, the employer generally cannot make unilateral changes to the employee's obligations.

In general, employment terms and conditions that have been agreed upon by employer and employee can only be amended by a written agreement of both parties. In the limited cases where an employer is allowed to unilaterally amend the employment terms and conditions agreed upon by the parties the employer must have legal grounds for such changes, must notify the employee two months in advance of any changes, and follow other formalities prescribed by law.

Employment-related Orders

Employers in Russia are required to issue an internal order each time an employee is hired, transferred to a new job, granted vacation, disciplined or terminated, and in certain other cases. For example, Article 68 of the Labour Code expressly requires that the order on hiring must be issued and presented to the employee for countersigning no later than three days after the employee has commenced work. When an employment agreement is terminated for any reason an order on termination must be issued and presented to the employee for countersigning on the last day of employment (Article 84.1 of the Labour Code).

Labour Books

The labour book is the principal document containing a formal record of a person's employment history and certain other information. The employer must make a record of employment in its employees' labour books in respect of any employment exceeding five days.

The labour book is vital to each employee because it confirms his/her right to a state pension and other social benefits. Employers are responsible for keeping their employees' labour books (if this work at this employer is the employee's primary employment) and making all records in them in a timely manner and in strict conformity with the required format. The employer must return the labour book, duly completed and stamped, to the employee on the last day of employment.

Mandatory Policies and Procedures

All employers in Russia are required to issue Internal Labour Regulations and other mandatory labour-related policies and procedures. All employees should familiarize themselves with these policies against their signature. This procedure is essential for the relevant policies, procedures and other mandatory requirements to become binding on the employees. The employer's policies and procedures should be issued in the Russian language (or in a bilingual version) and be approved by an internal order of the CEO of the company or head of the representative office/branch office.

Probationary Period

The employer has the right to establish a three-month probationary period for a newly hired employee. The employer may also set a six month probationary period for employees hired for certain top executive positions (e.g., head of an organization and chief accountant and their deputies, and head of a branch office, representative office, or other separate structural subdivision of an organization). The imposition of a probationary period must be specifically stated in both the employment agreement and the order on hiring. If during the probationary period the employer determines that the employee does not meet the criteria established for the role for which he/she was hired, the employee can be dismissed by the employer without payment of severance pay and with only three days' written notice.

Such notice to the employee must provide the reasons why the employee is deemed as having failed to pass the probation. The employee is also entitled to resign during the probationary period, without stating any reason, with three days' written notice to the employer.

Minimum Wage

Wages for full-time work may not be lower than the minimum monthly wage established by the applicable Russian legislation. The amount of the minimum monthly wage is periodically indexed by the government. The federal statutory minimum monthly wage as at the time of writing this book is currently RUB4,611 per month (approx. USD154).

Regional minimum wages are established by regional agreements. They apply to all employers in that region that do not opt out within 30 calendar days of the official publication of the respective regional agreement. Some of the constituent regions of the

Russian Federation, including the City of Moscow, have already implemented regional agreements on a minimum wage. Regional minimum wages are always equal to or higher than the federal minimum wage and are tied to the regional minimum standard of living. For instance, the minimum monthly wage in Moscow as of 1 January 2012 is RUB11,300 (approx. USD377).

Work Time

Employers are required to keep a record of all the time worked by each employee, including any overtime. The regular working week is 40 hours. Any time worked over 40 hours per week is classified as overtime and may only be demanded by employers in extraordinary circumstances, as specified in Article 99 of the Labour Code, and in most cases only with an employee's prior written consent. The Labour Code limits the total amount of overtime for an employee to 120 hours a year, and an employee cannot be required to work more than four hours of overtime over two consecutive days.

Overtime must be paid at a rate of 150% of the regular hourly rate for the first two hours of overtime worked in any one day, and at a rate of 200% of the regular hourly rate thereafter. Upon the employee's written request, the employer can compensate for overtime work by granting the employee additional time off in lieu of payment; the time off should be no less than the time worked as overtime.

It should be noted that certain limitations regarding overtime work apply to certain protected categories of employees, including employees under the age of 18, pregnant women, women with children under the age of three, disabled employees, and some other categories defined by federal laws.

Workers may also be hired on the terms of an open-ended working day. The primary advantage of this is that there is no need to obtain consent whenever the employer asks an employee to work overtime. Moreover, the extra hours worked by employees with an open-ended working day need not be paid as overtime: instead they are entitled to additional paid vacation of no less than three calendar days per year.

Nevertheless, it is important to note that employees with an open-ended working day can be required to work overtime only occasionally and upon a specific order of the employer when there is a need for such overtime work. Further, job positions subject to the open-ended working day regime must be approved by the employer and listed in the company's Internal Labour Regulations.

Chapter 19: Employment Rules in Russia

Holidays and Non-working Days

There are currently 12 public holidays in the Russian Federation. Uninterrupted weekly time off must not be less than 42 hours. As a rule, employees may only be required to work on a non-working day or public holiday in extraordinary circumstances, as specified in the Labour Code, and only with the employees' prior written consent. As a general rule, employees must receive payment at no less than twice the regular rate for any work performed on a non-working day or public holiday, or be given time off in lieu of payment.

Some limitations regarding working on public holidays and nonworking days apply to certain protected categories of employees, including employees under the age of 18, pregnant women, women with children under the age of three, disabled employees, and other categories as defined by federal laws.

Vacations

Employees in Russia are entitled to annual paid vacation of at least 28 calendar days per year of employment. An employee is entitled to use his/her vacation time in full once he/she has worked for the employer for at least six months. The Labour Code requires that the dates of the annual vacation of each employee be indicated in the vacation schedule for the calendar year, which the employer must approve by mid-December of the preceding year. The Labour Code further requires that employers notify their employees in writing at least two weeks before the commencement of the vacation. Each employee's vacation allowance should be paid at least three days before a vacation is due to start.

Sick Leave

Employees are required to submit a doctor's note for any absence only after their recovery and return to work. Generally, employees cannot be terminated by the employer while absent on sick leave, and are entitled to receive statutory sick leave compensation.

Sick leave compensation for the first three days of sick leave is covered by the employer, the rest of the term of sickness is covered by the Russian State Social Insurance Fund, which is funded by the employer's mandatory social contributions paid on a year-to-date salary of up to RUB512,000 (approx. USD17,067) in 2012 for each employee per calendar year. Since 1 January 2007, sick leave compensation and maternity leave compensation have been regulated by Federal Law No. 255-FZ On Obligatory Social Insurance in the Event of Temporary Disability and in Connection with Maternity (as amended), dated 29 December 2006. Pursuant to this law, sick leave compensation must be paid to an employee in the event of his/her illness or injury (labour-related or other) and when an employee is caring for a sick family member, as well as in some other instances.

The duration of payment and amount of sick leave compensation varies according to the grounds for the sick leave. In cases of labour related injury or occupational disease, the amount of sick leave compensation is 100% of the employee's average earnings. In other cases sick leave compensation is determined on the basis of the employee's average earnings and total term of employment.

Since 2011 the average earnings for the purpose of sick leave compensation are to be calculated with reference to the two calendar years preceding the year when an employee takes sick leave. In 2012 the statutory maximum average daily earnings for the purpose of sick leave compensation are RUB1,202.74 per day (approx. USD40), if the employee's overall employment term exceeds or is equal to 8 years. If the employee's total term of employment is less than six months, the sick leave compensation cannot exceed the federal minimum monthly wage.

If the employee has more than one place of employment and has been employed with the same employers for the preceding two calendar years, he/she is entitled to sick leave and/or maternity leave compensation at each place of employment and to child care leave compensation at one place of employment at the employee's choice. If the employee has more than one place of employment and has been employed with different employers for the preceding two calendar years, he/she is entitled to the above compensations only at one of his/her current places of employment at the employee's choice. If the employee has more than one place of employment and has been employed both with the current and with other employers for the preceding two calendar years, he/she is entitled to the above compensations either at each place of employment or at one of his/her current places of employment at the employee's choice.

Maternity Leave

Paid maternity leave consists of 70 calendar days prior to a birth, plus 70 calendar days after the birth. Further paid maternity leave is provided in the event of complications while giving birth or in cases of multiple births (86 and 110 calendar days after the birth respectively). Maternity leave is to be provided cumulatively; that is, if less than 70 days maternity leave are used before birth, the balance is added to the 70 days of paid maternity leave provided after birth.

Just like sick leave compensation, maternity leave compensation is paid out of the Russian State Social Insurance Fund, which is funded by the employer's mandatory social contributions. The amount of the maternity leave compensation is determined on the basis of the employee's average earnings and total term of employment.

Since 2011, average earnings are calculated with reference to two calendar years proceeding the year when an employee takes maternity leave. In 2012 the statutory maximum average daily earnings for the calculation of maternity leave compensation are RUB1,202.74 per day (approx. USD40). The maternity leave compensation is to be paid as a single payment. If the employee's total term of employment is less than six months, the maternity leave compensation cannot exceed the federal minimum monthly wage.

In 2012 women have the right to request the employer to calculate their maternity leave allowance based on a specific formula, effective until January 1, 2011. In this case an employee's average earnings for the purpose of maternity leave allowance should be calculated with reference to the last twelve months of work preceding the month when an employee takes maternity leave. The statutory maximum average daily earnings for the calculation of maternity leave allowance in this case are RUB1,136.99 per day (approx. USD38).

A child's care provider (the employee who has given birth or who is the father, grandmother, grandfather or other relative who is taking care of the child) may request partially paid childcare leave until the child is three years old. The employee retains the right to return to his/her job during the entire period of paid/unpaid leave, and the full leave period is included when calculating the employee's length of service.

The procedure for calculation of sick leave, maternity leave and child care leave allowances is rather complicated in Russia; it is highly recommended to verify the procedures and documentary requirements on a case-by-case basis.

Dismissal

An employment relationship may be terminated by the employer only on the specific grounds provided in the Labour Code, including; a reduction in the workforce, the employee's repeated failure to perform his/her employment duties without justifiable reasons (if the employee was lawfully disciplined within the preceding 12 months), the employee's unjustified absence from the workplace for more than four consecutive hours during one working day, and other reasons.

Arbitrary termination of an employment relationship by the employer is not allowed, except in the case of the company CEO, who can be terminated by unilateral decision of the owner provided he/she is paid adequate severance compensation, equal at least to three months' average earnings.

Employers must strictly comply with specific procedures and documentary requirements provided by the Labour Code when terminating employment for any reason. The Labour Code gives additional protection to a number of categories of employees, including minors, female employees, employees with children, trade union members, and various other categories. Conversely, employees are entitled to terminate their employment at any time, without stating any reason, and, as a general rule, with only two weeks' written notice to the employer.

Compensation

Salaries must be paid to employees at least once every fortnight. Employers are obliged to pay salary and other employment-related payments on the dates set by their internal labour regulations and by the individual employment agreement.

The employer is required to pay compensation (i.e., interest) for any delay in payment of salary and other employment-related payments in accordance with Article 236 of the Labour Code. In addition, employees have the right, upon prior written notice to their employer, to stop working if their employer delays payment of their salary for more than 15 days. Employees must be compensated in the currency of the Russian Federation (rubles). As a general rule, employment-related payments in a foreign currency (both in cash and by bank transfer) are prohibited.

Employment of Foreigners in Russia

Generally, when hiring foreign national employees employers must obtain:
1.   Permission to hire foreign nationals,
2.   Individual work permits and
3.   Work visas, before foreign nationals are employed and/or actually commence work in Russia (except for citizens of Belarus and Kazakhstan).

As a precondition for obtaining permission to hire and a work permit, a company must file an application for a quota for work permits. The application for a quota for the following year should be filed with the authorities before 1 May of the current year.

The above procedure equally applies to foreign nationals working in Russia under civil-law agreements for the performance of work or the provision of services (e.g., marketing consultants or sales representatives). Permission to hire, work permit and work visa requirements equally apply to representative offices and branch offices of foreign firms.

Foreign nationals working at accredited Russian representative offices or branch offices of foreign firms also need to obtain a personal accreditation card from the accrediting body of the representative or branch office in order to apply for a work permit and work visa. Generally a work permit and work visa are issued for a one year period.

The procedure and required documents vary according to whether or not the foreign national requires a Russian visa. In practice, the process of obtaining permission to hire foreign nationals, individual work permits and work visas in Moscow may take from four to six months to complete. In other regions of the Russian Federation this period may differ. Also employers are required to provide financial, medical and social guarantees in respect of their foreign employees in Russia and comply with the general migration monitoring requirements, including filing notifications of foreign employees' travel into and out of Russia, as well as within its territory.

Thus, employment of a foreign national in Russia requires advance planning to allow sufficient time for all procedures. The Russian authorities may adopt a list of quota-exempt professions/positions for each year, which allows employers to hire foreign employees without observing the quota requirement.

There is also a special category of foreign employees – the highly qualified foreign specialist (a "Specialist"). A Specialist is subject to a simplified procedure for obtaining a work permit and a work visa.

To obtain a work permit for a Specialist his/her employer is not required to obtain a quota to hire foreigners and permission to hire foreign employees. Representative offices of foreign firms cannot use this simplified procedure.

The main criterion for recognizing a foreign employee as a Specialist is the salary level paid in Russia. To satisfy this criterion, the salary received by the Specialist under a local employment /civil law agreement should be RUB2 million (approx. USD67,000) per year or more. A work permit and a work visa invitation letter are issued within 14 business days. The Specialist may receive a work permit and a work visa for up to 3 years.

Russian law provides for severe penalties for non-compliance with the above work permit and work visa requirements for foreign employees. During the past year the Russian government has made it a priority to increase control over the use of foreign employees in Russia. It has considerably extended regulation and tightened up enforcement of the above-mentioned migration law requirements.

Russian migration legislation is currently undergoing significant amendment, so the procedures involved could be modified at any time. It is highly recommended to verify the procedures and documentary requirements on a case-by-case basis in advance.

Chapter 20: Intellectual Property

Patents

An invention is a technical solution in any field related to a product (inter alia, to a device, substance, microbial strain, or cell culture of plants and animals) or a process. Patent protection is given to an invention if it is novel, inventive and industrially applicable. The maximum duration of patent protection for an invention is 20 years from the date of the application, subject to payment of annuities.

The term of a patent for an invention related to a medicine, pesticide or agrochemical, the use of which is subject to obtaining special permission, may be extended at the request of the patent owner for a period not exceeding five years. The right to obtain a patent belongs to the inventor, his/her employer (in case of an employee's invention) and their assignees. A patent application is filed with the Federal Service for Intellectual Property, Patents and Trademarks ("Rospatent"), which examines it and grants a patent if the invention meets the above-mentioned criteria.

A utility model is a technical solution pertaining to a device. Utility model protection is similar to that of inventions, with certain limitations and restrictions. A utility model is granted patent protection if it is new and industrially applicable. The term of a utility model's patent protection is ten years from the filing date of the application, subject to payment of annuities, and may be extended for an additional period not exceeding three years.

An industrial design is an artistic and construction solution that determines the outer appearance of a product of industrial or handicraft origin. An industrial design is granted patent protection if it's essential features are novel and original. An industrial design is deemed novel if the combination of its essential features does not comprise information publicly available in the world before the priority date of the industrial design. An industrial design is considered original if its essential features evince the creative character of a product's distinctive features. Industrial design patent protection is granted for 15 years, subject to payment of annuities, and with the possibility of extension for an additional period specified in the application, but not exceeding ten years.

Under Russian law it is possible to assign or license an invention, utility model and industrial design protected by a patent to another person. Such assignment and license agreements should be recorded with Rospatent, failing which the agreements are deemed null and void. These agreements enter into force as of the date of such recordation. The patent owner has the sole right to use an invention, utility model or industrial design that is protected by such a patent.

Without the patent owner's permission no one is allowed to use a patented object in any way, including importation, manufacture, application, offer for sale,

sale or other introduction into commercial turnover, or storage for this purpose. Infringement of patent rights may entail civil, administrative or criminal liability in accordance with the applicable legislation.

Trademarks and Service Marks

Under Part IV of the Civil Code, trademarks (service marks) are designations individualizing goods or services of legal persons and individual entrepreneurs. Legal protection of trademarks and service marks is granted by virtue of their registration with Rospatent or by virtue of international agreements to which the Russian Federation is a party. A mark may be represented by a word or words, pictures, three-dimensional signs and other designations or combinations thereof. A trademark may be registered in any colour or colour combination. Trademark and service mark protection is granted for ten years from the filing date of the application, and may be renewed during the last year of validity for a subsequent ten-year period.

Trademark and service mark registration is cancelled if the term expires without having been renewed. Trademark and service mark legal protection may be terminated upon a request from an interested party in respect of all or part of the respective goods and services due to non-use of the trademark or service mark during any continuous three year period after the registration date. Assignments and licenses of trademarks and service marks must be registered with Rospatent. In the absence of such registration they are deemed null and void.

Company Names and Trade Names (Commercial Designations)

Company names are designations that identify or distinguish different legal entities when conducting their commercial activities. Legal protection of company names is provided by the Civil Code and the Paris Convention for the Protection of Industrial Property, to which the Russian Federation is a party.

In the Russian Federation, a company name consists of two parts; the indication of a business's legal structure and the distinctive name of the company. A company may use the official name of the Russian Federation or any words derived there from in its company name only with the consent of the Russian Government. The right to a company name arises from the moment of state registration of the legal entity. The owner of a company name is allowed to use its company name exclusively, and to prohibit others from its unauthorized use.

The owner of a company name may not alienate its company name or grant the right to use it to another person. A legal entity may not use a company name that is identical or confusingly similar to the company name of another legal entity if both entities are engaged in similar business activities and the company name of the former legal entity has been incorporated in the state register of legal entities prior to state registration of the latter. A legal entity illegally using the company name of another legal entity is obliged to cease such use at the request of the company name owner and to compensate for any losses caused. A company name owner may use its company name or its individual elements as a part of its trade name or a trademark (service mark) belonging to the company name owner. A company name incorporated in a trade name or a trademark (service mark) is protected regardless of the protection of the trade name or the trademark itself.

Trade names are protected by virtue of the Civil Code. Part IV of the Civil Code contains a special section concerning legal protection of trade names. Trade names (so-called "commercial designations") are designations which individualize trading, industrial or other types of enterprises owned by legal entities and individual entrepreneurs.

Trade names differ from company names in that they do not require registration and are not subject to obligatory incorporation into the foundation documents of the trade name owners. The owner of a trade name enjoys an exclusive right to its trade name and may use it by any lawful means. The exclusive right to a trade name arises if the designation which is used as a trade name possesses sufficient distinctiveness and its use has gained notoriety within a certain territory. The scope of protection of a trade name used for the purpose of individualization of an enterprise located in the Russian Federation is limited to the territory of the Russian Federation.

An exclusive right to a trade name terminates if the owner of the trade name fails to use it during a continuous one-year period. A trade name owner may grant the right to use its trade name to another person under a lease of enterprise agreement or a franchising agreement.

Copyrights and Neighbouring Rights

Part IV of the Civil Code protects works of science, literature and the arts (copyright), and grants protection to the rights of performers, phonogram producers, broadcasting and cable-casting organizations, database compilers and publishers (Part IV of the Civil Code uses the term "publicators") (neighbouring rights). Copyright protection arises by virtue of the creation of a work of art without any registration requirements. An author enjoys personal (moral) rights (right of authorship, right to the name, right to public disclosure, right to protect the author's reputation) and proprietary rights (right of reproduction, distribution, import, public demonstration, public performance, translation, modification, etc.). Personal (moral) rights are inalienable from the author and cannot be assigned or transferred by agreement. The proprietary rights to a copyrighted object may be licensed or assigned by virtue of a copyright agreement.

Part IV of the Civil Code allows for the transfer of copyright in the form of an exclusive or non-exclusive license agreement as well as by an assignment of copyright. The term of copyright protection for all works, including software programs or databases, is the lifetime of the author plus 70 years after his/her death. The author's moral rights (right of authorship, right to the name and right to protect the author's reputation) are protected perpetually. Infringement of

144

copyright may entail civil, criminal or administrative liability.

Software Programs and Databases

Copyright protection also applies to software programs and databases. Pursuant to Part IV of the Civil Code, software programs are protected as literary works, while databases are protected as compilations. Although registration is not mandatory for protection, an author may optionally register and deposit software or a database with Rospatent.

A software program or a database is protected for the lifetime of the author(s) plus 70 years after his/her (their) death(s). The right to use a software program may be granted under a software license agreement.

Chapter 21: Natural Resources (Oil and Gas/Mining)

Today Russia is one of the largest mineral producers in the world. Russian mineral resources are an important component of its wealth.

Russia differs from other countries where the private ownership of minerals in the ground exists and where land owners have title to all mineral resources located below their land plots. All Russian subsoil resources in the ground, including oil, gas, gold and other minerals, unless extracted, are owned by the Russian state, irrespective of who holds the title to the relevant land plot or holds the relevant subsoil license. Rights to extract subsoil resources can be granted under subsoil licenses which, as a rule, provide that ownership rights to the extracted resources belong to the holder of the relevant license.

Subsoil Legislation

The Constitution of the Russian Federation stipulates that subsoil-use legislation falls within the joint competence of the federal and regional state authorities. However, in practical terms the regional authorities have competence over deposits of certain commonly occurring mineral resources and insignificant subsoil plots.

The core legal act in the mining and oil and gas domain is the Russian Federation Law on Subsoil

Resources dated 21 February 1992, as amended (the "Subsoil Law"). The Subsoil Law provides the general legal framework for the use of subsoil resources in Russia and covers almost all principal issues connected with geological survey, exploration and production/mining of underground resources.

The other principal law governing the use of subsoil resources in Russia is the Federal Law on Production Sharing Agreements dated 30 December 1995, as amended (the "PSA Law"). The PSA Law sets forth the legal framework for Russian and foreign investments in the geological survey, exploration and production of subsoil resources.

The principal piece of legislation regulating operations with precious metals and gem stones in Russia is the Federal Law on Precious Metals and Gem Stones dated 26 March 1998, as amended (the "Precious Metals Law"). The Precious Metals Law provides the general legal framework for the processing, use and disposal of precious metals and stones, and has specific provisions on geological survey, exploration and mining of such metals and stones.

Subsoil Users

Under the Subsoil Law both Russian and foreign companies may hold subsoil licenses in the Russian Federation, save for licenses for strategic deposits, which may be developed by Russian companies only. The user of off-shore fields may only be a Russian company that is at least 50% owned by the Russian state and which has at least five years' experience of development of off-shore fields. Although foreign companies are allowed to hold subsoil rights in respect of nonstrategic deposits, in practice there are only a few cases where a foreign company directly holds subsoil rights in Russia. Therefore, foreign companies usually hold subsoil rights to Russian deposits indirectly through their Russian subsidiaries which are allowed to hold subsoil rights to on-shore strategic deposits.

Licenses

Russia, similarly to many other countries, has adopted a licensing system. Subsoil licenses in Russia include: geological survey licenses, exploration and production/mining licenses and combined licenses (geological survey, exploration and production/mining licenses).

A geological survey license may be granted for a maximum period of 5 years (10 years for off-shore fields) and can be extended if needed for completion of the works. Exploration and production/mining licenses and combined licenses can be issued for a term equal to the life of the project, however in practice they are usually granted for 20 or 25 year terms and can generally be extended provided there are no violations of the license terms and conditions by the license holder.

Geological survey licenses are issued without a tender or auction based on an application of the interested party. Unlike geological survey licenses, production/mining licenses and combined licenses can be granted only through a tender or auction, except

    1. when a production/mining or combined license is issued to a holder of geological rights that made a commercial discovery under a geological survey license and

    2. with respect to strategic deposits (subsoil plots of federal significance) included by the Russian Government into the list of strategic deposits to be licensed by decision of the Government without a tender/auction.

Subsoil licenses are issued by the Federal Agency for Subsoil Use (Rosnedra). Rosnedra is in charge of granting subsoil rights with respect to all onshore deposits, except for strategic deposits. Rights to strategic deposits may only be granted based on a decision of the Government of the Russian Federation.

Transfer of Subsoil Rights

Subsoil rights in Russia are not freely transferable. This means that they cannot be sold, pledged or otherwise encumbered. However, the Subsoil Law permits the transfer of subsoil rights in certain instances (except for the transfer of rights to strategic deposits to companies with foreign participation), which makes such rights transferable to a limited extent. Such instances include:

    1. transfer of subsoil rights from a parent company to its subsidiary and vice versa and transfer between the subsidiaries of the same parent company.

2.   transfer following a merger of the license holder with and into another company.
3.   transfer following a consolidation of the license holder with another company.
4.   transfer following a spin-off or split-off of a new company. Any such transfer of subsoil rights requires a special decision of Rosnedra. Rights to strategic deposits are not transferrable to companies with foreign participation unless otherwise is determined by the Russian Government for a specific deposit.

The above options are often used by subsoil users for structuring their business, as well as for the "sale" of licenses, which is only possible through a sale of the licensee's shares.

Strategic Deposits

In 2008 Russia introduced a long-discussed set of restrictions for foreign investors in respect of strategic subsoil plots (subsoil plots of federal significance). Strategic deposits include the following:

1. Subsoil plots containing deposits and showings of uranium, diamonds, high-purity quartz, the yttrium group of rare earths, nickel, cobalt, tantalum, niobium, beryllium, lithium, or the platinum group of metals (irrespective of the size of the deposits).
2. Subsoil plots containing the following reserves, as evidenced by the State Register of Reserves, as of 1 January 2006:

a. Recoverable oil reserves equal to or exceeding 70 million tons;

b. Gas reserves equal to or exceeding 50 billion cubic meters;

c. Hard-rock gold reserves equal to or exceeding 50 tons; or

d. Copper reserves equal to or exceeding 500 thousand tons;

3. Subsoil plots located in the inland sea waters, territorial sea waters, or on the continental shelf of the Russian Federation;

4. Subsoil plots that can only be developed using land used for defence and security.

The list of subsoil plots of federal significance is published by the Federal Agency for Subsoil Use and includes approximately 1,000 strategic deposits and is updated on a regular basis. It is noteworthy that the list is not exhaustive and any deposit that meets the above criteria will be deemed strategic irrespective of whether it is included into the list or not.

Production Sharing Agreements

In the Russian Federation production sharing agreements (PSAs) are used to provide a particular legal framework for foreign investors in the mining, oil, gas, and other extraction sectors. The main objective of the PSA legislation is to provide investors in these sectors with greater stability in fiscal and regulatory areas over the long term. The main legislation governing PSAs in Russia is the PSA Law.

Since 2003 subsoil plot development under the PSA Law has been available only if the subsoil plot was put out to auction and the auction failed. That is, only those plots that are not of interest to subsoil users on standard license terms and conditions may be developed under a PSA. Therefore the best deposits are distributed under subsoil licenses and the PSA regime is not very attractive to subsoil users.

Due to the above and to the PSA tax regime established at the same time, PSAs have, in practice, become largely ineffective in terms of attracting foreign investment into Russia.

Precious Metals and Gem Stones

Under the Precious Metals Law precious metals include gold, silver, platinum, palladium, iridium, rhodium, ruthenium and osmium; and gem stones include natural diamonds, emeralds, ruby crystals, sapphires, alexandrites, and natural pearl and unique amber formations. Both lists, of precious metals and gem stones, are exhaustive.

Precious metals, with the exception of native metals, may be refined by organizations included on a special list of companies authorized to do so, which is maintained by the Russian Government.

Following the refining process, precious metals may be sold on the domestic market. Export requires a separate export license, which in practice is usually granted to banks and major producers.

It is important to note that the Russian authorities enjoy a right of first refusal to purchase precious metals and gem stones from mining companies. The prices for precious metals in such instances are based on world market prices. The pricing of precious stones is carried out by expert commissions on the basis of world market prices.

Chapter 22: Financial and Legal Services in Russia

Russia has a young financial & legal services sector that offers a range of opportunities for international and domestic companies, particularly in the light of Russian Government plans to develop International Financial Centre in Moscow.

Although the Russian economy suffered from the recent financial downturn significantly the Government managed to weather the crisis relatively well protecting to a large extent the financial sector from its impact. As the economy is gradually recovering the performance of financial institutions is meliorating.

Russia has a lot of banks, nearly 1000 by the central bank's last count but the sector is dominated by state owned leviathans: the top 30 banks, of which many are at least part owned by the state, account for 75% of total banking sector assets. Foreign banks have very little market share. And Russia's largest bank, Sberbank, is in a class of its own, owning 26% of all assets and a half of all retail deposits.

Non-banking sector (investment funds, insurance companies, private pension funds) is rather small yet it has demonstrated steady development throughout 2010 – 2011. Thanks to the growing stock market non-state pension funds and investment funds managed to attract significant resources recently. The insurance sector driven primarily by the demand in mandatory insurance products is also promising. Motor, property and voluntary health insurance are expected to continue to grow while life insurance market is still miniscule. The 10 leading insurance companies control about 45% of the insurance market and are highly diversified in all segments. Overall insurance penetration remains very low.

Russia's two main stock exchanges, MICEX and RTS, signed a binding merger agreement in June 2011 (USD 5 bln deal value). MICEX is in the top 20 exchanges (World Federation of Exchanges) while RTS's largest market is FORTS, or Futures and Options RTS.

The legal services market in Russia is growing. With legislation becoming more complex and sophisticated and a larger number of transactions being ruled by English Law, international firms, primarily British, are very much in demand especially in areas such as international financing and M&A.

Key opportunities

The Russian market opens up a wide range of commercial opportunities for foreign firms across the sector:

Banking: Russia is in need of more efficient banking practices, in particular on lending priorities, risk management, data processing and insolvency rules.

Legal Services: In the context of M&A Activity, privatisations, dispute resolutions, litigation and arbitration expertise in English Law is in greater demand.

Accountancy: With the increased business activity and strengthening of the regulatory regime foreign expertise in auditing as well as recognised international professional certification are the most in demand.

Insurance and Pensions: The reform of the insurance and pensions industry is a key concern for the Russian government. There is an opportunity to showcase foreign experience and expertise particularly in private sector pensions.

PPP: Given the major infrastructure projects planned for the next decade the Russian government is keen to develop PPP projects. There is an opportunity to showcase UK experience and expertise.

According to the Russian legislation foreign credit organizations wishing to do business in Russia can either set up (or purchase) a Russian legal entity or open a representative office. The latter presupposes performance of a limited range of functions which exclude any entrepreneurial activities. Foreign credit organizations are prohibited from acting via their branch network in Russia and are to choose one of the above mentioned options.

Credit organizations are subject to accreditation and licensing by a relevant authority. There are also minimum capital requirements for banking and non-banking entities (banks RUB 180 mln (2012), insurance companies RUB 120 mln (2012), private pension funds RUB 50 mln).

Special attention is paid to the foreign investors' activities in the insurance sector where there is a 25% quota for foreign participation. The quota is determined by a ratio of total capital owned by non-residents in entities with foreign investments to the total capital of entities registered in Russia and operating in the sector. Once the quota exceeds 25%, the regulating authority stops issuing licenses to insurance entities that are subsidiaries of foreign companies or have over 49% of foreign participation in their capital.

Chapter 23: Pharmaceuticals and Healthcare Sector in Russia

The protection of citizens' health is one of the principles of the constitutional system of Russia declared by the Russian Constitution, and the Russian healthcare system is built around this principle.

The formal basis of the Russian healthcare system is laid out in Federal Law No. 323-FZ On the Fundamentals of Citizens' Health Protection in the Russian Federation (the "Fundamentals"), which completely replaced its predecessor, Fundamentals of the Legislation of the Russian Federation on Protection of Citizens' Health, No. 5487-1, dated 22 July 1993, from 1 January 2012.

The Fundamentals, which are still not fully in force, standardize healthcare and significantly restrict the marketing and promotional activities of pharmaceutical companies. Federal Law No. 178-FZ on State Social Care, dated 17 July 1999, as amended (the "Social Care Law") is also an important legislative act regulating the Russian healthcare system.

The main legislative act specifically governing the pharmaceutical market in Russia is Federal Law No. 61-FZ on the Circulation of Medicines, dated 12 April 2010, as amended (the "Law on Circulation of Medicines"). To date, no specific law has been passed that separately regulates medical products aside from two articles in the Fundamentals, though an attempt to pass such a law was made and a new law is currently being discussed.

Other laws that are also important for the pharmaceuticals and healthcare sector include Federal Law No. 184-FZ on Technical Regulation, dated 27 December 2002, as amended, governing technical regulation, namely the declaration of conformity of medicines and certification of medical devices and medical equipment (the "Law on Technical Regulation"); Federal Law No. 38-FZ On Advertising, dated 13 March 2006, as amended (the "Law on Advertising"), governing advertising of medicines, medical equipment, medical products and medical services; and Federal Law No. 99-FZ On Licensing Certain Types of Activities, dated 4 May 2011, as amended (the "Law on Licensing"), governing licensing in the Russian Federation.

Regulatory Bodies

The regulatory bodies governing the healthcare system and pharmaceutical market of the Russian Federation are the Ministry of Healthcare and Social Development (the "MOH"), the Ministry of Industry and Trade (the "MIT") and the Federal Service for Surveillance in Healthcare and Social Development (the "Federal Service").

The MOH is responsible for drawing up state policy and regulation in healthcare, circulation of medicines for human use, social development, protection of consumers' rights and in other rather numerous areas.

160

The MOH submits drafts of federal laws and acts of the President and of the Government on healthcare to the Government. The MOH also adopts a significant number of important executive regulations on circulation of medicines required by laws.

The MOH, among other things, also:

1. Adopts general pharmacopeial monographs, and publishes state pharmacopoeia.
2. Registers medicinal preparations for human use (control is performed by the Federal Service).
3. Issues permits for the conduct of clinical trials (control is performed by the Federal Service).
4. Issues permits for importation of a specific lot of unregistered medicines for their clinical trials, their expert examination for the purposes of state registration, and for rendering medical aid to a patient if he or she has extremely serious indications.
5. Registers maximum manufacturers' prices of medicinal preparations included into the list of essential and most important medicinal preparations, also known as the essential drug list (ED List, or EDL).
6. Attests qualified persons at medicine manufacturers.

The MIT, among other things:

1. Plays an important role in the procedure for declaration of conformity of medicinal preparations.
2. Grants licenses for the manufacture of medicines.

3. Keeps a register of licenses granted.

The Federal Service, among other things:
1. Exercises control over: pre-clinical trials of medicines, clinical trials of medicinal preparations (being medicines in medicinal forms), quality and manufacturing of medicines, production of medicinal preparations, storage, transportation and importation into the territory of the Russian Federation, advertising, sale, and destruction of medicines and use of medicinal preparations,
2. Exercises control over the prices of EDL medicinal preparations.
3. Monitors the assortment and prices of EDL medicinal preparations.
4. Monitors the safety of medicinal preparations;
5. Grants licenses for pharmaceutical activities;
6. Keeps a register of licenses granted.

Clinical Trials of Medicinal Preparations and Medical Tests of Medical Products

The Law on Circulation of Medicines, similarly to its predecessor, contains a broad definition of clinical trials. It defines clinical trials as a study of the diagnostic, therapeutic, prophylactic, and pharmacological properties of a medicinal preparation in the process of its administration to humans and animals, including the study of the processes of its absorption, distribution, modification, and excretion, using scientific methods for the purposes of obtaining.

1. Evidence on the safety, quality, and efficacy of the medicinal preparation;
2. Data on adverse reactions of humans and animals; and
3. Data on the effects of its interaction with other medicinal preparations and/or food products/ animal feed.

According to the Rules of Clinical Practice in the Russian Federation, adopted by Order of the Russian Ministry of Healthcare No. 266 dated 19 June 2003, a clinical trial is a study of the clinical, pharmacological and pharmacodynamic effects of the studied medicine on humans, including processes of absorption, distribution, modification and excretion, for the purposes of obtaining, through scientific methods of assessment, evidence of the efficacy and safety of medicines, and data on anticipated side effects and on the effects of interaction with other medicines.

Manufacturing

According to the Law on Licensing, the manufacture of medicines is a licensable type of activity. The licensing procedure is governed by the Regulation on Licensing the Manufacture of Medicines, approved by Government Resolution No. 684, dated 3 September 2010. A license for manufacturing medicines is valid for an indefinite term.

As a general rule, only registered medicines may be manufactured in Russia. The manufacture of medicines is prohibited in the following cases:

1. The manufacture of medicines that are not included in the state register of medicines, except for medicines that are manufactured for the performance of clinical trials and for exportation.
2. The manufacture of falsified medicines.
3. If the manufacturer does not have a license for manufacturing medicines; and
4. The manufacture of medicines in breach of the rules for organization of the manufacture of medicines and quality control.

Importation

In accordance with the Law on Circulation of Medicines, importation of medicines may only be performed by:
1. Manufacturers of medicines for their own manufacturing purposes.
2. Foreign developers of medicines or foreign manufacturers of medicines, or other legal entities as their representatives for the performance of clinical trials, state registration of medicinal preparations, inclusion of a pharmaceutical substance into the state register of medicines, and quality control of medicines subject to the permission of the Federal Service.
3. Organizations carrying out wholesale of medicines.
4. Scientific-research institutions, educational institutions of higher professional education or manufacturers:
   a. For development of medicines,

b. for trials of medicines,
c. for control of medicines' safety, quality and effectiveness subject to the permission of the Federal Service;
5. Medical organizations and other organizations mentioned for the purposes of rendering medical assistance to a specific patient if he or she has extremely serious indications, subject to the permission of the Federal Service.

Importation of medicines into the Russian Federation is governed by the Rules of Importation of Medicines Intended for Medical Use, adopted by Resolution of the Russian Government No. 771, dated 29 September 2010. In addition, since Russia together with Kazakhstan and Belarus formed the Customs Union, decisions of the Commission of the Customs Union are binding on all members of the Customs Union, In accordance with Decision No. 748 of the Commission of 16 August 2011 (which came into force from 1 October 2011), importation licenses for properly registered medicinal preparations are effectively abolished on the territory of the Customs Union. This marks a significant change in the way the medicines enter the territory of the Russian Federation. However, this measure is only aimed at reducing the amount of paperwork done by the relevant authorities and will not affect the mechanisms for control of imported medicinal preparations. This control will be performed directly at the stage of customs procedures in relation to these medicinal preparations.

Imported medicines are released onto the Russian market only after, inter alia, their conformity to applicable Russian requirements is confirmed. In this regard it is important to note that mandatory certification of medicines was replaced several years ago with a declaration of their conformity. This change caused a significant reaction in the Russian pharmaceutical market since a procedure aimed at minimizing state involvement in the pharmaceutical market turned out to be quite burdensome for foreign pharmaceutical manufacturers.

Importation of medical products is performed in the ordinary course of importation. Imported medical products are released into the Russian market only after, inter alia, they are duly certified. It should be noted that certification of all medical products in Russia is performed according to the rules for certification of electrical equipment established in Decree of the Russian State Committee on Standardization and Metrology No. 36, dated 16 July 1999.

Wholesale

Pursuant to the Law on Licensing, pharmaceutical activity (including wholesale, retail sale and preparation of medicines) is a licensable type of activity. The licensing procedure is governed by the Regulation on the Licensing of Pharmaceutical Activities, approved by Resolution of the Russian Government No. 416, dated 6 July 2006, as amended. A license for the performance of pharmaceutical activity is valid for an indefinite term.

Wholesale of medicines is currently governed by the Rules for Wholesale of Medicines, approved by Order No. 1222n of the Russian Ministry of Healthcare, dated 28 December 2010.

Wholesalers of medicines may sell medicines or place them at the disposal of the following legal entities and persons:
1. Other organizations carrying out wholesale of medicines;
2. Manufacturers of medicines for manufacturing purposes;
3. Pharmacy organizations;
4. Scientific-research institutions for scientific research purposes;
5. Individual entrepreneurs having medical or pharmaceutical activities licenses; and
6. Medical organizations.

Only duly registered medicines can be sold on the territory of the Russian Federation. Russian law explicitly prohibits the sale of falsified, poor quality and counterfeit medicines. An accompanying document must be executed for each particular medicinal preparation, stipulating, inter alia, the medicine's name (international non-proprietary name and trade name), expiration date, information on the manufacturer, supplier, buyer, etc.

The wholesale of medical products is not a licensable activity in Russia, unless the medical equipment in question is of any special type, e.g., X-ray medical equipment. In the latter case wholesale of the medical equipment will require a license for activities involving sources of ionizing radiation.

Retail Sale

Retail sale of medicines is regulated by the Rules for the Sale of Medicines in Pharmacy Institutions, Fundamental Provisions (OST 91500.05.0007-2003), approved by Order No. 80 of the Russian Ministry of Healthcare, dated 4 March 2003, and by the Order on the Sale of Medicines, approved by Order of the MOH No. 785, dated 14 December 2005.

Retail sale of medicines is exercised by pharmacy organizations, individual entrepreneurs having a pharmaceutical activities license, and medical organizations and their separate subdivisions located in rural settlements where there are no pharmacy organizations.

Pharmacy organizations include pharmacies (selling ready-to-use medicinal preparations, production pharmacies, and production pharmacies having a right to produce aseptic medicinal preparations), pharmacy stations and pharmacy kiosks.

Prior to 2011 there existed a list of over-the-counter medicines and all other medicines, by default, had the status of prescription medicines. That list was abolished by virtue of Order of the MOH No. 1000an, dated 26 August 2011. Now sellers should dispense medicines exclusively in accordance with the instructions on their use.

Pharmacy institutions and individual entrepreneurs having a pharmaceutical activities license need to comply with a requirement for the minimum assortment of medicinal preparations necessary for rendering medical aid. The current minimum assortment of medicinal preparations is established by Order of the MOH No. 805n, dated 15 September 2010.

Similar to wholesale activity, retail sale of medicines is subject to licensing and only registered medicines can be sold in the Russian Federation.

Retail sale of medical products is not a licensable activity in Russia, unless, as in the case with wholesale, the medical equipment in question is of any special type.

Price Regulation

The basis for the system of state regulation of the prices of medicines and its most general rules are set forth in the Law on Circulation of Medicines.

Under the Law on Circulation of Medicines and Government Resolution No. 865 On the State Regulation of Prices of Medicinal Preparations Included in the List of Essential and Most Important Medicinal Preparations, dated 29 October 2010 ("Resolution 865"), the price of medicinal preparations included in the EDL is controlled by the state, and is subject to state registration and mark-up regulation.

Price control of EDL medicines is an important tool used in the organization of the healthcare system, ensuring that essential and most important medicines are accessible for all citizens. The current ED List was established by Government Ordinance No. 2199-r, dated 7 December 2011. By law, revision of the EDL should be an annual process.

According to the Law on Circulation of Medicines, the state regulation of prices of medicines included in the ED List is effected through the following measures:
1. State registration of the maximum manufacturer's prices of medicines (done at the federal level); and
2. Establishing maximum wholesale and retail trade margins applied to the prices of medicines (done at the regional level).

Technical Maintenance of Medical Equipment

Technical maintenance of medical equipment is a licensable type of activity according to the Law on Licensing. The licensing procedure is governed by the Regulation on Licensing Technical Maintenance of Medical Equipment (Except When Such Activity Is Carried Out to Satisfy the Own Needs of a Legal Entity or Private Entrepreneur), approved by Resolution of the Russian Government No. 32 dated 22 January 2007, as amended, which is also to be replaced due to adoption of the new Law on Licensing in 2011. A license for the maintenance of medical equipment is valid for an indefinite term.

It should again be noted that in certain cases (similar to the licensing of manufacturing of medical equipment) a license for technical maintenance of medical equipment alone is not sufficient and other licenses may be additionally required in order to lawfully conduct technical maintenance of certain types of medical equipment (e.g., a license for activities involving sources of ionizing radiation is necessary when X-ray equipment is being serviced).

Promotion

The only type of promotional activity in the pharmaceuticals market that is currently specifically regulated by Russian law is "advertising". Russian legislation contains few provisions that specifically regulate practices (other than simple advertising) aimed at the promotion or marketing of medicines. This means that, in order to determine the rules applicable to such things as seminars, hospitality, entertainment and similar activities, in most cases one has to refer to the generally applicable provisions of Russian law.

Advertising is defined in Article 3 of the Law on Advertising as "information spread by any means, in any form, and by any media, which is addressed to an indefinite circle of persons and aimed at drawing attention to the object advertised, at creating or maintaining interest in it, and at promoting it in the market." The Law on Advertising contains general restrictions on advertising that are as applicable to medicines and medical products as they are to any other product. The general requirement is that the advertising should be fair and true. However, the Law on Advertising also contains specific provisions applicable to medicines and medical products.

Under the Law on Advertising, prescription medicines, as well as medicines that contain narcotic or psychotropic substances approved for medical use, treatment methods, and medical products and equipment that require special training for their use may only be advertised in specialized printed publications intended for medical and pharmaceutical professionals and at medical or pharmaceutical events.

The Law on Advertising contains a requirement that the advertisement of medicines, medical services and medical equipment must be accompanied by a warning regarding contraindications against their use and application, the necessity to read the instructions on their use, or the necessity to consult a specialist. This requirement, however, does not apply to advertisements disseminated at medical or pharmaceutical events and contained in specialized printed publications for medical and pharmaceutical professionals and to other advertisements where the recipients are solely medical and pharmaceutical professionals.

The Law on Advertising further introduces a group of restrictions that apply to the advertising of medicines. Thus, the advertising of medicines should not:
1. Be addressed to minors.
2. Contain references to specific cases of recovery from disease or improvement of

health as a result of the advertised object being used (except in advertising exclusively for medical and pharmaceutical professionals).

3. Contain expressions of gratitude from individuals in connection with the use of the advertised object (except in advertising exclusively for medical and pharmaceutical professionals).

4. Create an impression of advantages of the advertised object by reference to the fact that the trials required for its state registration have been conducted.

5. Contain statements or assumptions that consumers have certain diseases or impairments of health.

6. Facilitate the impression that a healthy person needs to use the advertised object (this prohibition does not apply to medicines used for prevention of diseases).

7. Create an impression that one does not need to consult a physician.

8. Guarantee the positive effect of the advertised object, its safety, effectiveness and absence of side effects.

9. Represent the advertised object as being a dietary supplement or other product that is not a medicine.

10. Contain statements that the safety and/or effectiveness of the advertised object are guaranteed by its natural origin.

Chapter 24:
Telecommunications Sector in Russia

Applicable Laws and Competent State Bodies

The general rules in the telecommunications sphere in the Russian Federation are established by the law "On Communications" dated 7 July 2003 (the "Communications Law"). The Communications Law governs communication activities in the Russian Federation and assigns certain policy and regulatory functions to various bodies. The Communications Law also establishes a separate procedure for licensing and certification in the sphere of telecommunications.

State regulations on the provision of services and other telecommunication activities are to be drafted by the President, the Government, and the Ministry of Telecommunications and Mass Communications (the "MTMC") the federal governmental authority for communications.

The MTMC is the state body responsible for the preparation of draft federal laws, presidential decrees and government resolutions in the area of communications and information technology. The MTMC is also entitled to issue its own regulations, such as setting out requirements for the use of numbering capacity, regulations on the use of radio frequencies, rules for providing communication services to subscribers, etc.

The other state agencies in the sphere of telecommunications are; the Federal Service for Supervision in the Sphere of Telecommunications, Information Technology and Mass Communications ("Roskomnadzor") and Rossvyaz – the Federal Communications Agency (the "FCA").

Roskomnadzor is responsible for exercising day-to-day control in the area of communications and mass media, monitoring the use of the frequency spectrum, registration of frequency assignments, mass media registration, issuance of licenses in the area of communications and mass media, and the protection of personal data.

The FCA is responsible for coordination of international and federal programs in the area of information technology and communications, the numbering capacity of operators, certifying the compliance of equipment, and organizing the operation, development and modernization of the federal communications and national information and telecommunications infrastructure.

The MTMC also organizes the work of the State Commission for Radio Frequencies (the "SCRF"). The SCRF is made up of representatives of various ministries and state bodies. The main tasks of the SCRF are to coordinate use of the frequency spectrum by different state bodies and frequency spectrum allocation. The SCRF is responsible for the allocation and use of the frequency spectrum, scientific and technical research in the area of use of the frequency spectrum, frequency spectrum demilitarization / conversion, technical policy for use of the frequency spectrum, and also with regard to electromagnetic compatibility. Any decision of the MTMC, Roskomnadzor or the FCA may be appealed in court.

Communications Networks

The Communications Law establishes that the unified communications network of the Russian Federation consists of the following categories of communications networks, located on the territory of the Russian Federation:

1. Public switched telecommunications network ("PSTN").
2. Dedicated communications networks.
3. Technological communications networks; and
4. Special purpose networks and other communications networks for data transfer with the use of electromagnetic systems.

The PSTN is designated for the provision of telecommunication services for a fee to any user of communication services on the territory of the RF. The PSTN network is connected to the PSTN's of foreign countries.

A dedicated communications network is designated for the provision of telecommunication services for a fee to a closed user circle or groups of such circles. A dedicated communications network doesn't have a connection to the PSTN and to the communications networks of foreign countries.

The technological aspects of a dedicated network's construction can be determined by the owner of the network. A dedicated communications network can be connected to the PSTN if the dedicated communications network complies with the requirements of the PSTN.

A technological communications network is designed to support the operational activity of enterprises and management of the technological processes used in operations. A technological communications network doesn't have a connection to the PSTN, and can be connected to the technological communications networks of foreign enterprises only for the execution of a unified/joint technological operation. A technological communications network can be connected to the PSTN with its re-categorisation to the PSTN, if this technological communications network complies with the requirements for the PSTN.

A special purpose communications network is designated for state needs, national defence, state security and law enforcement. Such a network cannot be used for the provision of services for a fee.

Telecommunications Licenses

Communication services can only be provided on the basis of a license. Among the communication services subject to mandatory licensing are the following:

1. Local telephone communication services (with or without services via public telephones, points of public access).
2. Telephone services provided via dedicated communications networks.
3. International and domestic long-distance telephone communication services.
4. Telegraph communication services.
5. Personal calling services.
6. Radio, cellular, or satellite communication services.
7. Provision of communication channels.
8. Data transmission services (including or not including VoIP).
9. Telematics services.

A license may be obtained upon an application. The license should be issued based on the results of an auction or tender in the following cases:

1. A communication service requires use of radio frequencies, and the SCRF determines that the radio frequency spectrum, available for provision of communication services, limits the possible number of communications providers on the territory;
2. Limited resources of the PSTN on the territory (i.e., limited numbering capacity resources) and the number of communications providers on the territory should be limited.

A decision on whether to issue a license is taken by Roskomnadzor within 30 days after the filing of the application. If during provision of communication services it is proposed to use radio frequencies, including for the purposes of television and radio broadcasting; or to perform cable television broadcasting, wired sound broadcasting, transfer voice data, including through a data transfer network, provide communication channels which go either beyond the territory of the constituent territory of the Russian Federation or beyond the territory of the Russian Federation, or to provide postal services, Roskomnadzor should decide on whether to issue a license within 75 days from the date of the filing of an application. Licenses are issued for a term of up to 25 years.

Roskomnadzor collects a fee for issuance of a telecommunications license in the amount of RUB2,600 (approximately USD87). The territory for which the license is valid is specified in the license. There are no restrictions on the number or type of communications licenses that a single licensee may hold.

The Communications Law does not permit the transfer of a license or any rights from the licensee to another person. The license can be reissued by Roskomnadzor only to a legal successor of the licensee.

Roskomnadzor has the right to terminate a license without applying to the courts if the operator is liquidated, or ceased its activities as the result of reorganization (except for reorganization in the form of transformation), or applies for termination of the license.

The license may be suspended if Roskomnadzor discovers a breach of law or of the conditions of the license by the operator, or non-performance of services for more than three months, or non-performance of services from the date specified in the respective license as the date for commencement of provision of services.

Rights to Use Radio Frequencies

The Communications Law provides transparent and open frequency allocation procedures and for a national frequency allocation table. Allocation of the frequency spectrum is organized in accordance with the Frequency Allocation Table, which has to be reviewed at least once every four years.

If a communications provider intends to use radio frequencies for provision of communication services, it should comply with the requirements for allocation of radio frequency bands and assignment of radio frequencies and radio frequency channels prior to obtaining the respective communications license.

The procedures for allocation of radio frequency bands and assignment of radio frequencies and radio frequency channels are established by the SCRF and Roskomnadzor. A decision of the SCRF on radio frequency bands allocation and a decision of Roskomnadzor on assignment of radio frequencies and radio frequency channels are taken within 120 days following the date a respective application is made. Radio frequencies, radio frequency bands and channels are allocated for a term of up to ten years.

The use of the frequency spectrum is subject to a one-off fee for allocation of a radio frequency, plus an annual fee for use of the radio frequency. The Communications Law does not provide for the transfer of the right to use a radio frequency to another operator.

In case of violations of the terms and conditions set forth in a decision of the SCRF on allocation of a radio frequency or in a decision of Roskomnadzor on assignment of radio frequencies and radio frequency channels, these decisions may be suspended for the period required for elimination of such violation, but not for more than 90 days.

As a general rule, a telecommunications provider that intends to use a radio frequency spectrum must obtain a resolution of the SCRF on allocation of radio frequency bands and a resolution of Roskomnadzor on assignment of radio frequencies and radio frequency channels. The only exception in the applicable legislation is virtual telecommunications providers who are not required to obtain the said resolutions since they use the networks and radio frequencies of other providers based on network cooperation schemes agreed upon between the providers.

Registration of Radio Frequency Emitters

Telecommunications facilities and equipment emitting radio frequencies are subject to registration. The authority responsible for such registration is Roskomnadzor. The relevant legislation includes a list of equipment subject to registration (most radio transmitting equipment) and some exclusions from the registration procedure (for example, cellular phones, DECT phones, Bluetooth, etc.)

A necessary condition for issuance of a registration certificate is obtaining decisions of the SCRF and Roskomnadzor on allocation and assignment of radio frequencies.

A decision on whether or not to issue a certificate should be taken within ten days. The term of the registration certificate corresponds to the term of the frequency allocation/assignment permit. If such a permit is not required a certificate may be issued for a term of up to ten years.

Broadcasting of Mandatory Public TV Channels and Radio Stations

Communications providers perform the broadcasting of mandatory public TV channels and radio stations on the basis of agreements with the broadcasters of such channels and stations.

A list of providers for broadcasting mandatory public channels and stations is approved by the President of the Russian Federation. Currently Federal State Unitary Enterprise "Rossiiskaya Televisionnaya i Radioveschatelnaya Set" is the only authorized

provider. The list of mandatory public TV channels and radio stations is set by the President of the Russian
Federation and currently includes eight TV channels and three radio stations.

The requirements on broadcasting mandatory public TV channels and radio stations on a free of charge basis (at the expense of the provider) are included into the licensing requirements to be complied with by communications providers rendering broadcasting services.

Mass Media Regulation

Applicable Laws and Competent State Bodies Broadcasting activity in the Russian Federation is governed by the Law "On Mass Media" of 27 December 1991 (as amended) (the "Mass Media Law") and the Communications Law. The Mass Media Law regulates activities in the sphere of broadcasting and sets requirements for the mass media.

The state authority exercising control over broadcasting is Roskomnadzor. Roskomnadzor registers mass media and issues licenses for broadcasting activities.

Another state authority in the sphere of mass communications is Rospechat the Federal Agency for Press and Mass Communications. Rospechat provides state services and manages state property in the sphere of the press and mass media.

Mass Media Registration

Under the Mass Media Law mass media covers printed periodicals, web periodicals, TV and radio channels and TV, radio and video programs, newsreel programs, and other forms of regular distribution of information under a permanent name. Mass media established on the territory of the Russian Federation are subject to registration by Roskomnadzor.

Foreign companies have limited rights to establish mass media:

1. A foreign company or a Russian company with a foreign share participation of 50 % or more may not found TV and radio channels and TV, radio and video programs;

2. A foreign company or a Russian company with a foreign share participation of 50% or more may not be a founder of a company broadcasting to an area which is more than half of the territory of the Russian Federation and/or which is home to more than half of the population of the Russian Federation.

For registration purposes an applicant must submit the following
documents to Roskomnadzor or its territorial agency:

1. An application for state registration of the mass media. Applications are accepted from legal entities, duly registered on the territory of the Russian Federation.

2. A copy of the documents certifying payment of the registration fee (for the whole of Russia – RUB6,000 and RUB3,000 for one territorial unit (approx. USD200 and USD100)).
3. Identification documents and documents confirming the registration address of an applicant (if the applicant is a Russian citizen).
4. Identification documents and documents confirming the right of permanent residence of an applicant in Russia (if the applicant is a foreign citizen or an apatride).
5. Foundation documents of an applicant (if the applicant is a legal entity).

An application should be filed with the service if the mass media products are to be distributed throughout Russia. If the distribution of such products is to be limited to the territory of one region, city or district, the application should be filed with the territorial division.

1. Extract from the shareholders register or participants register (if the applicant is a legal entity) in case of establishment of TV and radio channels and TV, radio and video programs;
2. Documents confirming the right to use the domain name of the Internet site in case of establishment of a periodical on the Internet;
3. The charter of the mass media editorial board or the agreement between the mass media founder and the editorial board (chief editor);
4. Documents confirming the transfer of the rights and obligations of the mass media founder to a third party.

The review period is normally 1 month. The registration certificate should be issued for an unlimited period of time. The founder of the mass media has the right to start the manufacture of the mass media products within one year from the date of issue of the certificate. If it misses the prescribed term the mass media registration certificate shall be deemed invalid.

The grounds for refusal to register mass media are limited to the following:

1. If the application was filed on behalf of a person or legal entity that does not have the right to establish the mass media in accordance with the Mass Media Law.
2. If the application contains false information;
3. If the name, tentative theme and (or) specialization of the mass media may be deemed abuse of the freedom of the mass media as determined by the Mass Media Law.
4. If the responsible authority had already registered mass media with the same name and form of transmission.

A refusal to register mass media should be provided in written form and specify the grounds for refusal as foreseen by the Mass Media Law.

The application may be returned to the applicant without review in the following cases:

1. If the application was filed in breach of the requirements of the Mass Media Law.

2. If the application was filed by an unauthorized person.
3. If the state registration fee was not paid.

Issues Arising out of Mass Media Establishment

A Russian legal entity conducting such business activity would require not only mass media registration but also to establish an editorial commission and the necessary staff. An editorial commission is the organization or persons manufacturing and editing the mass media. The founder of the mass media should approve a charter for the editorial commission of the mass media and (or) enter into an agreement with its editorial department. In addition, if there is more than one founder, a founders' agreement is required.

Chapter 25: Aerospace Sector in Russia

Aerospace is one of the Russia's highest value adding manufacturing sectors, with between 275 and 300 aerospace companies, including 108 industrial producers, and 111 R&D and design bureaus. Russian Aerospace industry experiences high level of state involvement and receives notable investment and support from the Government.

State Involvement

Federal budget spending on a State Programme to develop Russia's aviation industry is planned to amount to 1.7 trillion rubles in by 2025, which is stated in the draft program prepared by the Industry and Trade Ministry.

The Programme envisages that sales of Russian airplanes are to account for 10% of the world market, while helicopter sales are to account for 27%-30%. The share of domestic components are to account for at least 70% of the cost of airplane production by 2020–2025.

The Programme is divided into 7 subsectors:
1. Civil aircraft building.
2. Helicopter building.
3. Engine building.
4. Aviation equipment building.
5. Aviation aggregates building.

6. Science and technology.
7. Automated aircraft.

Governmental investment plans:

MC-21 and SSJ - 1,5-10 bln RUR per year per project up to 2015;

Tupolev-204SM and Beriev-200 - 37 mln RUR in 2012-2013 and then stop financing the projects.

The key industry players are:

United Aircraft Corporation (UAC) A holding consisting of the leading Russian aircraft design and manufacturing companies focused on the country's aircraft output and improving efficiency.

State Corporation Russian Technologies is designed to assist Russian organisations-developers and manufacturers of high technology industrial products in their development, production and exports by providing support in domestic and foreign markets and attracting investments to different industries including defence industrial complex.

One of its aviation assets is Russian Helicopters Holding. The managing body of the consolidated Russian helicopter industry, incorporates 14 helicopter companies, setting new standards of competitiveness, efficiency, technology, and profitability.

Central Aerohydradynamic Institute (TsAGI)

TsAGI is the first scientific institution to combine basic studies, applied research, structural design, pilot production and testing.

The Institute participates in several joint research programs on the development of next-generation aircraft covering such areas as structural strength, finite element method analysis, and optimization of structural weight. The next generation of TsAGI aircraft is conceptualized to have a life of 50,000 - 60,000 flight hours. TsAGI established contacts with a majority of research and development centres and aircraft manufacturers in Europe, the United States and Asia.

Key opportunities

Current projects and support

Russian Government has switched its priority to civil aircraft building. A number of indigenous aircraft programmes are underway or being planned that present opportunities for companies with contract research and/or consultancy capabilities:

MC-21 (Irkut Corporation, Yakovlev Design Bureau)

Tu 204SM (Tupolev)

Samolet 2020 (Ministry for Industry and Trade, UAC, TsAGI; at a discussion stage now)

Sukhoi SuperJet and MC-21 are predicted to occupy only 6.6% of the world market. To improve the figure Russian Ministry for Industry and Trade plans to launch a new project "Samolet 2020". Within the framework of this project it is planned to launch relevant avionics and business jet programmes alongside. Government plans to invest 120 mln RUR into market research and 100 mln RUR will be invested into compiling a required technological base for the project carried out by TsAGI.

The following areas are indicated by key industry players as fields for potential cooperation with foreign companies:

1. Pre-competition cooperation
2. "Green" solutions
3. Innovative sources of energy
4. for engines
5. Unmanned aircraft
6. Composite materials
7. Quality control in operation
8. Scientific cooperation
9. New generation IT technologies

Helicopters

The Russian Helicopter industry is now focused on light weight helicopters, as the Russian helicopter fleet abandons heavy vehicles and lacks the light ones.

Russian Helicopters is the leading Russian full-cycle designer and manufacturer of helicopters for civilian and defence markets. The holding actively works with international suppliers and seeks new partners in the following areas:

1. Modernization of manufacturing facilities.
2. Engineering service.
3. Complex solutions for projects.
4. Joint R&D.
5. 2-4 TRL level cooperation.
6. Innovative helicopter equipment.
7. Automated control systems.
8. Navigation systems.
9. Flight management systems.
10. Composite technology (not supply).
11. Search and rescue equipment.
12. Automated control systems.

Advanced Composites

Composite materials including power composite machines are in the focus of Russian Aerospace industry representatives' attention. New projects emerging in the Russian Aerospace sector envisage the use of advanced composite materials. UAC has announced a new $100m JV to manufacture composite wing components in the city of Kazan, Tatarstan. At the inception phase, the JV would import raw materials for composite components.

Aerocomposite Ltd, created by UAC, deals with design, testing, manufacturing and realisation of composite parts, aggregates and components of civil aircraft. It cooperates with British companies and is eager to find new partners.

Ulyanovsk Special Economic Port Zone

Creation of Special Economic Port Zone (SEPZ) can be of interest for companies who wish to manufacture close to their client or localize in Russia. The Ulyanovsk region ranks 1st in Russia in civil aircraft manufacturing. Investor support and international cooperation is welcomed now for the new project-creation of SEPZ.

Benefits for residents
1. Exemption from customs duties, VAT and excise taxes; property tax for 5 years; land tax for 5 years.
2. VAT refund for goods/equipment placed in SEPZ.
3. Profit tax rate reduction to 15.5%.

Chapter 26: Gift Sector in Russia

With a population of 142 million, Russia is the eighth largest retail market in the world and remains an attractive proposition for exporters and investors. It is also one of the fastest growing markets; Russia's GDP growth in 2011 was 4.3%.

Driven by the growing prosperity of the population, the giftware market in Russia continues to grow across all sub-sectors. Pre-recession growth rates vary from 10% in tableware sector to 30% in fine jewellery. The latter continues to grow during recession. The market is far from saturation and major players are planning retail expansion. The value of individual gifts is growing; the average gift purchase is now about **£50 while the upper end is going above £500**.

Imports dominate the market accounting for 80% to 95% of the market share. Major suppliers of mass market products are China and India. Upper market is dominated by European goods. Only 5% is taken by Russian made products, mostly of "national character". 'Made in the UK' is perceived as high quality and enjoys popularity among Russian consumers.

Key opportunities

Tableware

High quality tableware has traditionally been a sign of prestige and prosperity in Russia. Today practically all famous European brands are present in the Russian market - Herend, Meissen, Royal Copenhagen, Spode and Wedgwood, etc. However, newcomers are welcome. Distributors working in sectors such as household appliances or souvenirs keep expanding their range and enter the tableware market. British companies can particularly succeed in the high end of the market, that is dominated by European import from Czech Republic, Germany, France, Italy, Japan and the UK. 90% of the porcelain products are imported.

Fine jewellery

Fine jewellery has traditionally been very popular with Russian women; however, due to very strong competition from plenty of local manufacturers and high import duties this market is more difficult to penetrate. Nevertheless, official imports account for approximately 15-20% of the Russian fine jewellery market.

Major opportunities exist in the fashion/designer jewellery. Well established fashion brands (Yves Saint Laurent, Christian Dior, etc.) as well as new designer brands (Loree Rodkin, Robert Wa Tahiti, Steven Webster, etc.) are successful in the market.

Costume jewellery and accessories

Costume jewellery and accessories is a growing opportunity in Russia. If before costume jewellery was considered as low end products or something for young generation only, now more and more Russian women tend to buy costume jewellery across all price levels. Local production of costume jewellery is virtually non-existent.

Another opportunity is branded jewellery chains developed on a franchise basis.

Home Decorations

'Made in the UK' interior accessories enjoy big popularity in Russia and are sold in interior salons alongside furniture. Steven Shell (UK), Old Java (Indonesia), PD Global (UK), Tom's Drag (Germany), Kroemer (Germany), Coach House (UK), and many others are in the market already.

Business gifts

The business souvenir market is considered to be one of the most dynamic ones in Russia growing at 30%-35% every year. 95% of business souvenirs are imported. Exporters can be successful in the luxury segment where quality, image and brand are more important than price.

Chapter 27: Rail Sector in Russia

A Western company that comes into Russia expecting to apply its "standard approach" will not likely last long; it is simply too important to understand and adapt to local conditions. A foreign company trying to go it alone will likely run into problems and local partners are highly recommended.

Related to that, shortage of labour may be a problem for foreign companies. Overall, there is a shortage of qualified specialists in the rail sector in Russia today, and foreign companies should not expect to be able to simply hire necessary labour in Russia. It is more likely that foreign companies will need to partner with a local company that already has the necessary specialists on staff.

A wide range of opportunities exist within the Russian rail sector. Russia operates the world's 2nd largest rail network, with 85,500 km of track across what is the world's largest landmass. The Russian rail transportation market is entering the most interesting phase since creation of the Russian Railways in 2002. This phase should bring the market to the level of mature competitiveness.

In recent years, the wagon park has been actively renewed because a competitive market and a favourable investment climate had been formed in this sector. The volume of cargo railcar manufacturing in 2011 surpassed the wildest expectations. Russian wagon building plants manufactured 62,800 cargo railcars which is 24.4% more than 2010.

Russia is going through the positive changes in the manufacturing sector through the development of high-speed rail. Joint ventures Transmashholding/Alstom and Siemens/Sinara have been created in order to overcome the lag in technology of the Russian machine building sector.

The key company is Russian Railways JSC (RZD), rail monopoly, a vast organisation comprising 987 enterprises and 165 subsidiaries. It is Russia's fourth largest company by revenues. It is one of a few companies in Russia, whose expenditure on scientific and technical research may be compared to that of foreign corporations in terms of percentage of revenue.

Russian Railways started its 28 year reinvestment and modernisation programme in 2002. It is planned to last until 2030 and during this period it is anticipated that some £276 billion investment will be injected into the company for:

1. Overhaul, renovation and modernisation of existing track network.
2. Extension of network by additional 20.000 km.
3. Rolling stock replacement programme including short, medium and long distance locomotives and wagons and suburban electric trains.
4. Roll-out of High Speed network principally throughout Europe and Russian.

Modernisation of Russia's 350 major stations (at major cities and at all cities with population over 200,000) incl. development of facilities for Hi-Speed, of multi-modal hubs and rail hubs and also modernisation of Moscow's 8 Heritage stations.

Currently Russian Railways is going through the stage of partial sale (10-15%) through an IPO with an estimated starting price of $10-15 billion. 54 subsidiaries are to be sold before 2013. The experts have no doubt that there will be a lot of investors.

Key opportunities

Station Modernisation and Property Development Programme

There are some 350 stations in the Russian Railways (RZD) network and among them some 8 heritage type older stations in central Moscow.

Currently RZD are heavily involved in modernisation of Russia's 81 major stations (at major cities and at all cities with population over 200,000 pople) including development of facilities for high-speed, of multi-modal hubs and rail hubs and also modernisation of Moscow's 8 Heritage stations.

The programme envisages modernisation of 332-400 stations by 2015. In 2010 the company estimated the total cost of the programme as RUR 30 billion (£625 million) but last year they understood that construction of a logistics centre in Ekaterinburg's station alone will cost them about RUR 10-30 billion.

Therefore, private investors will be undoubtedly involved in cost breakdown.

Finance and Legal

RZD is preparing its assets for a partial sell-off of 10-15% of the company with an estimated starting price of $10-15 billion mooted to take place between 2013 and 2015. Observers forecast enormous interest from investors. The specific approach to the sale will be determined later. At the moment, the following options are being discussed; selling to a strategic investor, an Initial Public Offering on a designated exchange/ combination of these two options. Either of these options would require a colossal amount of work on the part of government officials and the management of RZD that could potentially provide a pipeline of new projects for foreign finance and legal sector firms.

Last October, a 75% shareholding in Russian Railways' largest subsidiary Fright One was sold for a record sum of RUR 125.5 billion (£2.6 billion).

Safety and Security

Russian Railways is actively striving to implement a comprehensive programme of public safety in transportation. In 2011-2013 the company plans to allocate RUR 1.9 billion (GBP 39.5 million) to spend on equipment and security systems for the most important public rail facilities. Public safety is a priority for the Russian Government as well. In 2010 it allocated RUR 4 billion (GBP 83.3 million) to the sub-programme Rail Transport Security 2010-2013 from the Russian Federal budget.

Energy Efficiency and Intelligent Transport Systems

Russian Railways is keen to implement energy-saving technologies especially within the framework of RZD Stations Modernisation Programme (mid-term investment budget for 2011-2013 is RUR 9.9 billion (GBP 206.2 million). Russian Railways' specialists are studying foreign expertise (project management) in the area of efficient use of complex intelligent systems providing comfort (temperature, efficient ventilation, humidity, lighting, communication), safety (prevention of flooding and fire); security (stable electrical facilities, control over passenger traffic flow inside the building, alarm systems), as well as reducing running costs. The opportunities for foreign companies in this area are enormous because there are not many companies able to develop complex solutions on such a scale in Russia.

High speed rail and World Cup 2018

Russian Railways supported by the Russian Government plans to establish high-speed rail roads between the cities which will host the games of the football World Cup in 2018. The realisation of this project will cost RUR 5.5 trillion (GBP 114.5 billion) and will by definition involve the introduction of innovative foreign technologies. At the moment Russian Railways is striving to elaborate a complex plan of transport system supply and interaction of different transport types during the event itself.

Overall, the government has already spent over RUR 330 billion (GBP 6.8 billion) on the development of the railway industry over the last three years. According to the open sources, the estimated cost of the Moscow St Petersburg high-speed line construction will be financed by a private investor who will invest RUR 205 billion (GBP £4.2 billion). The investor has not been chosen yet.

Nanotechnologies

RZD is also seeking to introduce the innovative use of nanotechnologies. The company plans to start implementing nanotechnology on railroad transport that will help to enhance the quality of transport services, as well as increase volumes of traffic and travelling speeds. Nanotechnology products are planned to be used in the construction of new railways stations (heat insulating, non-combustible materials).

Corporate Education

Russian Railways invests in corporate education. The education programmes include financial management and operational efficiency, change and innovation, external environment and others. As per the latest development plan of RZD, RUR 1 billion (GBP 20.8 million) or 0.46% of planned revenues will be invested in corporate education in 2012. By 2015 the company plans to increase this figure to 1%.

Chapter 28: Construction Industry in Russia

In 2011 construction activity in Russia has grown by 4.5%. In 2012 the Russian economy and its construction industry are expected to perform better than the global average, and substantially better than those of Western Europe.

In 2012 the investment volumes into Russian real estate will reach £4 bn exceeding pre-crisis levels (£3.2 bn in 2008). In the next 5 years the volume of housing construction in Russia is to grow by 1.5 times, from 58 to 90 million square metres; over the next decade Russia will spend £173 bn to double the rate of road building.

2011 saw record investment volumes into Russian real estate with growth of over 170% above the level reached in 2010 and exceeding £5.3bn.

The Russian construction industry has resumed growth in 2011 posting 4.5% output increase. Only in July 2011 construction was up 17.6% year on year, it's strongest for two years. Such vibrant growth was last seen more than three years ago during the construction boom.

The growth is attributed not only to increased private investment in commercial, industrial, infrastructural and residential construction projects, but also to a series of upcoming events during which Russia will play host to the world including the

1. Asia-Pacific Economic Cooperation (APEC) Summit 2012.
2. The Winter Olympic Games 2014.
3. The FIFA World Cup 2018.

Key opportunities

Moscow Expansion

The Moscow city government have announced an ambitious plan to annex 144,000 hectares (395,000 acre) to the city's current territory and build 60 million square meters of housing and 45 million square meters of commercial real estate on new lands in the next 20 years. In effect, the Moscow area will more than double its size. The Moscow authorities will seek international expertise in order to develop a scheme for the first major expansion of the Russian capital in 50 years.

The Moscow expansion plan will create opportunities for foreign experts in urban planning, architectural and engineering design, environmental planning, project management, cost consultancy and transport planning.

Skolkovo Innovation Centre

In 2010 the Russian Government announced its plans to establish the Skolkovo Innovation Centre; the modern centre for research and development. The construction commenced in the second half of

2011.The plan is to develop the Russian Silicone Valley for 25,000-30,000 people on the territory of 380 hectares. The construction is planned to conform to international green-construction standards making it a flagship for Russia. The project paves way for both energy-efficient building designs and a "green" waste-processing programme. The cost of construction of the Skolkovo innovation city is estimated at £2 - 2.4bn by 2015.

Hospitality

The Russian hospitality market saw robust growth in 2011 with Moscow city government announcing ambitious plans to build 40 new hotels by 2012 and over 300 by 2025. These trends are also demonstrated by regions outside Moscow and Saint Petersburg, where both domestic and foreign investors are gradually exploring the potential of other major Russian cities, such as Krasnodar, Kazan, Yekateringburg, Samara, Kaluga.

Sochi-2014

Russia will host the XXII Olympic and XI Paralympics Winter Games in February – March 2014 in Sochi. The potential opportunities for foreign companies are enormous. The official delivery plan records some 218 projects to be constructed in Sochi. More than £ 20 bn will be spent on the preparation for the 2014 Winter Olympic Games.

There has been particular interest identified in foreign companies offering innovative products and services in the area of architectural design, civil engineering and construction. While the construction of sport facilities is nearing completion ample opportunities for construction companies still exist in the hospitality sector.

World Cup 2018

Russia's FIFA World Cup 2018 will generate large opportunities for foreign business in the sector of construction. The plan suggests construction of 13 new stadiums in cities across the country, as well as renovation of three existing ones. The Russia's federal budget will provide over £6 bn of funding for the FIFA World Cup 2018 sports infrastructure. The biggest spending is planned after the year 2013.

Retail

The Russian retail market remains rather unsaturated. However, steady sales growth and rising competition for consumers have piqued retailers' interest in new mall formats. In 2011 Russia remained in the top league of Central and Eastern European countries with the highest level of retail space development. Out of 146 shopping centres under construction in Europe in July 2011, Russia accounted for 19. Nearly one fifth of the first half of 2011's European development total, just over 400,000 sq m, was completed in Russia. Moscow accounted for 36% of that new space with the opening of AFIMALL City and two other shopping centres.

Industry experts estimate that the Russian shopping centre pipeline for 2012 is about 3 mn sq m, of which 25% will be constructed in Moscow and the surrounding region. Large cities outside the Moscow and Saint-Petersburg Regions attract increasing interest of developers and retailers due to reasonable rents in sought-after locations and the level of deficit in terms of shopping centre space.

Residential

Residential real estate is set to grow as well with the Russian government's agenda to increase the volume of housing construction in Russia up to 90 m sq m per annum by 2015.

A new system of so called Self-Regulating Organizations (SRO) has been introduced in 2010 replacing the issuance of licenses for construction and designing in Russia. SROs are the unions/associations of builders and designers. SROs issue permits to their members, enabling them to proceed with their business activities namely with works in engineering survey, preparation of project documentation, construction, reconstruction, major repairs of capital construction facilities, which have impact on safety of capital construction facilities.

Federal environment and technology organization Rostechnadzor has given SROs a right to issue Competency Certificates to a specific type of work. The Competency Certificates can be granted without time limitations for work/activity for both domestic and foreign companies.

Chapter 29: Power Sector in Russia

Russia's power industry has recently been transformed beyond recognition from a state owned monopoly into liberalized industry. With transformation still underway, the sector offers exciting opportunities to foreign companies expanding overseas.

With total installed capacity worth 229 GW, Russia is one of the largest power markets in the world; every year energy production and consumption in Russia continues to grow. The market share is dominated by thermal production with 69%, followed by nuclear with 16%, and hydro with 15%. Russia has 31 nuclear reactors distributed over 10 sites. This number is expected to reach 42-58 by 2030 at a rate of 3-4 per year as of 2015. Russia is trying to rethink its approach to power and create new power model which will allow reconfiguring the approach to baseload and peakload power and construction of additional grids.

Russia is also looking at energy efficiency sector reform; all of that offers potential opportunities to foreign business in such areas as engineering consulting, equipment upgrading and supplies, Smart-Grid and Smart metering technology. Additionally, turbines, valves, pumps and wiring are often on the tender lists.

Key opportunities

According to the three steps Energy Strategy, by 2030 the Russian Government plans to invest in the following projects; total investment is expected to reach $2000bn:

1. **Developing power capacities (2013-2015):** Russia is investing £40bn in nuclear reactor dissembling of nuclear waste management.
2. **Transmission:** £48bn investment is planned in construction of new power transportation lines and renovation of the existing facilities.
3. **Improving energy efficiency (2015-2022):** Russia annually invests at least £1million in energy efficiency.
4. **Developing renewables (by 2030):** Russia is planning to install wind power systems with a total capacity of 5000MW by 2020.

Tendering in the power sector in Russia has become more open and transparent in recent years. Major power companies have specialised departments or e-commerce platform responsible for procurement. However, there are still some barriers, such as tender information is available only in the Russian language plus there might be formal differences in technical regulations. A foreign company trying to go it alone will likely run into problems and local partners are highly recommended. In addition to local partners, friendly relations with the local administration in whatever region one plans to do business are also important. Background research and relationship-building are key.

Chapter 30: Ports Sector in Russia

The increasing volume of import/export operations at Russia's ports is enhancing the prospects for the ports' development with resulting opportunities for foreign companies.

Currently there are 64 seaports in Russia providing over 60% of the country's foreign-trade freight traffic. The majority of the Russian ports were established in 1960-70's therefore their technical state does not meet the 21st century requirements for water depth at berths and in water areas. 31 seaports are shallow with maximum service capacity at 10 thousand tons deadweight and only 10 Russian ports can accommodate modern vessels over 50 thousand tons deadweight. The only seaport that can service the vessels with deadweight over 150 thousand tons is Murmansk.

In 2010 the cargo turnover in the Russian ports was 526 million tons delivered by 187 thousand ships, with 211.6 million tons of dry cargo (mostly coal, metals and fertilisers) and 314.4 million tons of bulk liquids (predominantly oil).

According to the RF Ministry of Transport reports, by 2016 the Russian seaports will increase their cargo turnover by 46% (compared to 2010) and will reach 770 million tons. The biggest growth (three times by 2016) is expected in the container handling capacities

(3.4 million TEUs handled in the pre-crisis year of 2008).

The increasing volume of export/import operations encourages potential investors (both Russian and foreign) to pay more attention to the prospects of ports' development. The Russian Government adopted strategic programmes (e.g. the Russian Transport System Development Programme for 2010-2015) to enhance investment attractiveness, support serious upgrades of existing ports and construction of the new port areas.

14 billion roubles (£298 million) were invested in the Russian ports development in 2010. According to the federal programmes, 430 billion roubles (£9.15 bn) will be invested in the ports development projects by 2015; 300 billion (£6.4 bn) of which will come from non-budgetary funds. The port projects will be actively utilizing the PPP scheme of development. Attraction of large volumes of private funds will bring a demand for substantial development and improvement of the concessions, leasing mechanisms and legal basis. Russian government believes participation in such projects could be also interesting for foreign investors.

The port of Ust-Luga (a greenfield project) is becoming a key Russian port on the Baltic Sea. Upon full completion it will have 191 mln ton/year turnover (11.8 mln tons in 2010). The port will be able to serve vessels with the displacement tonnage of up to 150,000 tons and up to 17 meters draft. The volume of investments in the Port of Ust-Luga in 2012-2015 will exceed 249 billion roubles (£5.3 bn), out of which 15.2 bn rbls (£323.4 mln) will be allocated from the federal budget and 39 bn rbls (£829.4 miln) by the Russian Railways. The port development projects are carried out jointly with foreign companies.

A new deep seaport of Taman (the Azov-Black Seas region) will provide 100 million tons turnover by 2030 (dry cargo). The port of Taman will service the ships with a draft of 14 meters (46 feet) and with a displacement of 100,000 tons. The overall volume of investments will be 150 billion roubles (£3.2 bn), two thirds of which will be private investments. Possibility of a foreign port management company is now being considered.

Increasing gas exports promote development of new transportation facilities. One of the main projects in this area is the construction of the port complex for LNG transfer in the Gulf of the Ob River, Arctic region ("Sabetta") with 30 mln ton/year capacity by 2020. The new Arctic port investments (including transport and logistics infrastructure) are estimated in 900 billion roubles (£19.1 bn). The first LNG tanker is expected to leave the port in 2018. The project will be financed from the federal budget, Novatek (Russia) and Total (France). Another 2-3 foreign companies will probably join the main shareholders group (with a share of foreign capital up to 49%). Foreign companies are also invited to take part in the port and LNG plant development and construction.

The future plans include construction of the hub-port in the Kaliningrad region with the aim of serving the international transport corridors and an annual capacity exceeding 130 million tons of cargo, which will be able to compete with the largest European hub-ports, such as Rotterdam, Antwerp and Hamburg. The cost of project is estimated as 263 billion roubles (£5.6 bn). Final decision on the new port location will be made in 2012.

Based on the strong state support Russia plans to become one of the most important players in the world transhipment market by 2030.

Key opportunities

Technical upgrade of existing port facilities

Design and development of new marine terminals; rail container yards and other logistics facilities and infrastructure zones.

Port management

Development of the juridical basis and mechanisms for the PPP projects in the ports development sector.

Chapter 31: Conclusion

Many Russian businesses are dominated by a few all-powerful personalities and they love to send a middleman to handle face-to-face negotiations. Make sure you know just how much authority the person you are negotiating with actually has, don't expect to agree everything with the person across the table.

Often you will win a series of early concessions from your middle-man only to find he will back-track on them once he is spoken to the real power-broker. Make clear that these points are part of a package and re-opening them re-opens the rest of the deal too.

When you are dealing with lots of different parties at the same time, it can be common for one person to appear very friendly and reasonable but argue that the other players will never agree to your suggestions however much he would like to. This is most common when the other players are not present and is a ploy to try to extract concessions from you. Stick to your position.

Most Russian businessmen don't spend time on niceties, particularly when it comes to high-stakes deals. Don't be intimidated by their overly aggressive approach, or take it personally. Keep your cool and make sure you have a good local adviser who can take the flak on your behalf and steer you in the right direction.

Russian businessmen are chess-players and like to apply pressure on their negotiating partners by letting the clock run down with issues still unresolved. Deliberately delaying paperwork is a common tactic. Don't be afraid to get tough with them to resolve key issues and even call their bluff when necessary.

You can often be one of several parties all bidding for the same business. Make sure you can't be played off against your rivals by doing your research and understanding the relative strengths and weaknesses of your position.

You can think a deal is done then suddenly your negotiation partner will reveal a new piece of information at the 11th hour. Don't be shy about changing the terms of the deal to reflect this new information; you must protect your interests and not let these last minute surprises go unchallenged.

The Russian government wants more international business deals conducted under Russian law but the legislation is still not as comprehensive as English law, which is widely used internationally, in part because of the fairness and reputation of British justice. Stick to English law where appropriate you don't want a dispute heard in a Siberian backwater.

Five years ago when deals were being done at the drop of a hat in Russia, contracts were often pre-signed and emailed to people once contracts were ready to be exchanged. This left lots of room for error with the wrong contracts being used or loopholes left open. Now, insist on a 'wet ink' paper copy and read and sign every page.

Face-to-face meetings and getting to know potential business partners personally is an important part of Russian culture, as it is across Asia. Sometimes this can lead to lengthy dinners and entertainment. Never be tempted to re-open business negotiations save it for the boardroom and a clear head.

Good luck!